Growing older can be dangerous. The trail is treacherous, and the pitfalls are many. One is wise to be prepared. You know it's coming. It's not like God kept the process a secret. It's not like you are blazing a trail as you grow older. It's not as if no one has ever done it before. Look around you. You have ample opportunity to prepare and ample case studies to consider. If growing old catches you by surprise, don't blame God. He gave you plenty of warning. He also gave you plenty of advice.

Your last chapters can be your best. Your final song can be your greatest.

– Max Lucado
God's Inspirational Promise Book

Ease into Aging

PRAISES FOR EASE INTO AGING: THE GUIDE

Some of the best information available today regarding the aging process.

– Tom W.

* * *

As a life-long advocate of self-improvement, I could not believe how many new ideas I learned from this book.

– Jeff B.

* * *

Dick's new book empowered me to find greater purpose in my life at 70 by adding a brand-new job. Now I have way more money, more fun and new friends.

– Curtis N.

* * *

Dick's "words of wisdom" inspired me to implement many of the suggested life strategies that put me on the road to overall wellness. It's never too early to plan for the future.

– Donna S.

* * *

A great book full of life experiences!

– Vicki H.

* * *

This is a must- read book for absolutely every person, especially those between 35 and 55. Living the life you want- with safety, security and good health-is a lot easier if you make good decisions early. I believe this book fell into my lap just in time. It has helped formulate a plan for the critical changes needed so that I can live each to the fullest. Aging doesn't only happen when you're old-but planning can take a lot of the negative out of it, leaving your best days ahead.

– Bill C.

* * *

EASE into AGING:

The Guide

— Simple Yet Effective Strategies
for A More Peaceful and Productive
Approach to Life…
at Any Age.

by **DICK HARTMAN**
Author of *Motivating the Unmotivated*

DISCLAIMER

This book is not intended as a substitute for advice normally disseminated through a member of the medical or financial professions. It is solely intended as a source of suggestions and should be treated as such. One should always consult his or her healthcare or financial advisor before making any decision relevant to the medical or financial fields. The author specifically disclaims any liability for loss or risk, personal or otherwise, that is incurred as a consequence of the use or application of any of the contents of this book.

FIRST EDITION
Published in 2021
by Living Better Publishing

ISBN: 978-0-9619238-1-5

Library of Congress Control
Hartman, Richard Charles
Ease Into Aging: The Guide – *Simple Yet Effective Strategies for A More Peaceful and Productive Approach to Life…At Any Age.*
Control Number: 2020918852| December, 2020

Category: Motivational & Inspirational, Mid-Life, Self-Help, Aging, Guide

Written by: Dick Hartman | **www.DickHartman.com** | DickHartman2020@gmail.com

Edited by: Lee Caldecutt

Cover Concept by Casey Cleveland

Cover Designed & Formatted by: Eli Blyden Sr. | EliTheBookGuy.com

Printed and Published in the USA: Tampa Bay, Florida

*

*A portion of proceeds from the sale of this book
will be used to benefit the kids at*
ST JUDE'S CHILDREN'S RESEARCH HOSPITAL.

***

*If you love **Ease into Aging: The Guide,**
please go to www.Amazon.com,
enter **Ease into Aging: The Guide** or
scan with camera, the code below, and
write a review.*

Forever Grateful!
– Dick

WHO NEEDS THIS BOOK?
PERHAPS YOU DO!

If you are tired of living in the fast lane without being able to slow down; this is the book for you. If you feel like you're spinning your wheels and not accomplishing your goals and dreams, keep reading. Having feelings of uselessness and not belonging? You picked up the right book. Do you just want to uncomplicate your life and make it more enjoyable and manageable? Add this book to your cart.

Regardless of a person's age or stage in life, there are strategies you can follow to make your life the best it can be. And, you will find many of these great strategies in this guide. Chances are, since you picked up this book to check it out, you have been searching for ways to make adjustments in your life to have better control of it.

Welcome to a better future—starting today!

HOW AND WHY THIS BOOK WAS WRITTEN

I'm sure it wasn't an "ah-ha moment" but, after thirty-plus years of teaching others to be contributing members of society, I realized I was personally lacking many of the life skills needed for well-being and functionality in today's world.

One day, my adult son came to me and asked something like this: 'Dad, now that you're up there in years, is there anything you do, have done, or wish you would've done, that would slow down the aging process?'

Out of this innocent (I think) conversation was born *Ease into Aging: The Guide.* For the next few years I compiled and reorganized my own personal notes and blended them with the many strategies I have used over the years, turning them into this workable guide you are now reading. During this time, it became obvious that aging is a multifaceted physiological and psychological process that covers a wide range of issues. It also helped me realize there are many practices and habits we accept or allow during our younger years that adversely affect our later years. The biggest revelation is knowing that we have the ability to reverse (or at least minimize) many, if not most, of the challenges that arise from the process of living life.

So…Why did I write this book?

Since most people lead busy and complicated lives, I wanted to create an organized, easy-to-use book that would help guide and direct others in ways that make their lives easier and simpler, especially as they grow older. It takes a lifetime to experience and learn from the myriad pitfalls that people can face. So much stress and fear can be avoided simply by preparing how to address each issue (if it occurs), rather than scrambling in the moment. Or better yet–a person can adapt behaviors and perhaps avoid some of these pitfalls entirely! Despite the title, this information is beneficial for, and meant to be used by, individuals of all ages who want to lead a quality life. My hope is that *Ease into Aging: The Guide* will help you to:

1. Assess challenges you will most likely face as you move into each new chapter of life.

2. Identify strategies that will help, as the title implies, "ease" you into each new phase of life.

3. Recognize that you shouldn't wait to change actions and behaviors until you HAVE to. It's much easier to prepare for potential situations or concerns BEFORE they become an issue.

4. Understand that life doesn't have to be a major struggle at any age.

5. Avoid many of the pitfalls experienced by those who have preceded you.

Not everyone gets the opportunity to live a long and fulfilling life. Since you obviously plan to be one of the fortunate ones, know that you have the ability to vastly improve and enjoy the gift of the years you have been given. It's never too early to start…or too late!

Contents

PART THREE

CHAPTER TWELVE

EASE into AGING:

The Guide

*— Simple Yet Effective Strategies
for A More Peaceful and Productive
Approach to Life…
at Any Age.*

by DICK HARTMAN
Author of *Motivating the Unmotivated*

Introduction

Did you ever meet someone, assuming he or she was approximately your age, but later on discovered the person was actually many years older (or perhaps the opposite)? Now, more than ever, it is difficult to judge people solely by their appearance or the way they carry themselves. Why do some people seem to be much younger–or older? Some experts would say it's all in the genes. Obviously, genetics do have an effect on life, but that is only part of the story. The ongoing discussion of nature versus nurture seeks to determine which is more important to the well-being of the human race. It is becoming increasingly clear that, although your genetic makeup is a major component of how you look, feel, and age, all these factors can be altered by the way you live your life. In other words, you can overcome many genetic flaws or challenges, or at least minimize their effects.

And that's great news! We can actually improve most (if not all) aspects of our lives just by making adjustments to our lifestyle. We probably can't make all aspects perfect, but we *can* make them _better_. Some parts of our lives can be changed dramatically while others can only be improved nominally. Many factors come into play such as age, income, relationships, knowledge base, and commitments; each of us is different, and life affects each person differently. But the bottom line remains–we can all still make effective changes.

Ease into Aging: The Guide is addressed to those who want to live the best life possible and are willing to do what it takes to achieve it. You have, before you, over two hundred ideas, strategies, techniques and suggestions that can alter your life, or at least make it easier and more comfortable. Now is the time. It doesn't matter if you are in your 30s, 40s, 50s, 60s, or beyond. It is never too late…or too early to start.

It is important to be openminded and step outside your comfort zone as you navigate through many of these *strategies*. Although there are some that may never play a role in your life, there are many that will apply directly to you <u>*right now*</u>–and many more that will apply down the road.

The purpose of *Ease into Aging: The Guide* is two-fold. The first is to educate you regarding the pitfalls and challenges you could be facing as you progress. The second is to supply trigger points to get you started on your journey of self-improvement. With the aid of modern technology, you have more than enough information at your fingertips to revamp various aspects of your life. Keep in mind there is no one-size-fits-all approach. It is up to you to decide which strategies apply–and the best ways to apply them. The decisions that affect your life ultimately fall on your shoulders.

PREMISES

In order to understand and better utilize the life strategies presented in *Ease into Aging: The Guide*, it is important to embark on the journey with the following premises:

1. Life changes.

2. Most changes (not *all*, but *most*) in life happen slowly. It's usually better to deal with them sooner rather than later.

3. Many of these life strategies may pertain to you, but some may not. Many may not affect you now but could likely relate to your future.

4. Some of these strategies are simple and easy to implement; others are complicated and will take longer to incorporate.

5. **NO MEDICAL ADVICE SHOULD EVER BE TAKEN WITHOUT FIRST DISCUSSING IT WITH A TRUSTED MEDICAL ADVISOR.**

6. Many (if not *most*) of these *life strategies* will have more than one avenue for success. It is up to you to mold them to fit your world.

7. Many of the *life strategies* presented will affect your life in many different areas. Thus, they will appear in one chapter, but their outcomes could (and probably will) have a profound effect on many other facets of life.

8. It's best to be prepared for the unexpected things in life.

9. **NO FINANCIAL ADVICE SHOULD EVER BE TAKEN WITHOUT FIRST DISCUSSING IT WITH A TRUSTED FINANCIAL ADVISOR.**

10. Sometimes we can't make a "right decision." Sometimes we have to select the BEST decision and *make it right*.

11. Few things in this world are black-and-white absolutes. Most fall somewhere in the gray area.

Keeping these premises in focus will help you make better decisions as you apply these strategies. It will also help you weed out many of the unproven ideas that constantly bombard us from a variety of sources.

Part One

A ROADMAP FOR THE FUTURE:
PURSUING THE BETTER YOU

THE BEST WAY TO PREDICT THE FUTURE IS TO CREATE IT

– Peter Drucker
Creator of *the Drucker Theory of Business Management*

You may be at the point where you need to make decisions concerning how you want your future to unfold. It may seem daunting at times to project ahead. Oftentimes, we don't like to think about the future because we don't really know what lies five, ten, or twenty years ahead, and the unknown can be frightening. Obviously, we don't have total control of how our lives turn out, but we do have a say in how we approach it. Thus, we are able to make decisions now that will affect us in our later years. For this reason, it is important to consistently set and update goals so that we can arrive at where we would like to be. To this end, it is essential to have a workable plan for how to achieve our goals.

Many people believe they have plenty of time to plan for the future. They take for granted that they can 'work on it later.' Trust me, the future sneaks up on you. We all believe we will live long, productive, healthy lives and live happily ever after, but life has a way of taking some crazy, unexpected twists and turns. Some of these are easy to deal with but some can alter our futures forever.

Chapter One of this book enables you to perform an assessment of your life as you know it today. Be honest and don't be tempted to sugarcoat anything. It is important to complete **YOUR OWN** assessment based on **YOUR** life.

Chapter Two provides an opportunity to project how you want the future to look at different junctures. Depending on a person's age, an individual should plan and project in appropriate time increments, such as five, ten, or twenty years. A person may also consider using periods of one to two years, depending on the specific goals and the stage of life.

Chapter Three is where you will actually develop your plan of attack for the future, based on these assessments, while incorporating the strategies presented in Part Two. Many of these strategies should be put into action right away, particularly those that can be done easily. Others will need some research, preparation, or time to facilitate.

We can always have a wish list based on how we want our lives to turn out, but leaving it to chance is a huge gamble. Spending a little time making proactive, intentional decisions can forever alter your future.

Ease into Aging

CHAPTER ONE

TODAY IT ALL BEGINS:
WHERE ARE YOU RIGHT NOW?

Life is a journey with problems to solve and lessons to learn.
But most of all, experiences to enjoy.

– Anonymous

Your life, plans, goals, and dreams can be very different from those of others. Obviously, many people share similar ideas of what life should be, but each person not only has specific needs and desires for present-day living, but also how the future will play out. There is no cookie-cutter design for how life should be at any point. Sure, there are things that need to be done to secure our lives today and hopefully do so for the future, but people cannot and should not compare themselves to others who *are seemingly* at the same point in their lives.

Success is both elusive and multi-faceted. One can appear to be highly successful by one standard or frame of reference, but still be considered a failure by others. Even more importantly, the gauge of success is internal, and a person with myriad achievements may still judge himself as a failure by his own standards. Even the word "successful" is not defined the same way by all people and cultures. For some, success is based on financial positioning. For others, it is based on happiness. Still others measure success according to when their actions are consistently beneficial to others. All of these are important components in assessing achievement, but success can be so much more. Because it is based on personal standards and expectations, it is important to have a clear picture of what success truly means *to you*.

It's easy to be totally focused on the NOW part of life and taking care of *today*. What we need to avoid, however, is focusing all our attention on the *now* while avoiding making meaningful plans for the future. Each person is entirely capable of taking steps to solidify *today* while also addressing measures to create a concrete future.

First, let's talk about *today*. Steps should be taken to ensure a person is headed in the right direction. Using a baseball analogy, in order to steal second base, you first have to reach first base. This journey requires stamina, so the most important first step is to have a complete medical physical to ensure that you are healthy and have no underlying health issues. After scheduling and completing the physical exam, you should make sure you have one every year, making it a habit and a date on the calendar.

The next step to solidifying the present is to make sure you have an emergency fund to fall back on if anything affects your income stream. The financial experts suggest a person should put four to six months of income aside to cover living expenses as a hedge against the unexpected. This money should be stored in a readily available account, rather than in one that is difficult to access.

Another very important step is to plan consistent family time. Too many of us get bogged down in the everyday grind and don't spend enough time with those we care for the most.

One of the most important steps you should take for the present is to plan some ME time. This is time for you to do the things you enjoy doing.

> *(Author's note: As important as it is, ME time should never come before, or take the place of, family time. Through planning and scheduling, both can be easily achieved.)*

In the Appendix, you will find the ***Ease into Aging: Where I Am Today Assessment.*** Please take this assessment now, and be honest. Use as much detail as possible to paint an accurate picture of what your life is like at present. You will find the process very thought provoking. It will also be very helpful when making decisions for your future. In the event that you decide to consult with any advisors for additional information or planning, this information will assist these advisors to direct you toward good decisions that are customized to your unique situation. Don't be afraid to also solicit input from your close family members who have some "skin in the game," but remember you know your life better than anyone else does.

After completing the assessment, you will have a better picture of your life as it is today; this can be used as a reference on an as-needed basis. Keep this assessment available for periodic updates, goal setting, accountability, and to allow you to adapt. Life changes often.

CHAPTER TWO

THE FUTURE IS YOURS TO SEE: WHERE DO YOU WANT TO BE?

*I will do today what others won't,
so tomorrow I can do what others can't.*

— Jerry Rice,
NFL Hall of Famer

Now that you've completed the ***Ease into Aging: Where I Am Today Assessment,*** you should have a great snapshot of your life as it currently stands. That was the easy part. The purpose of Chapter Two is to help you conceptualize where you want to be in the future in most, if not all, phases of life.

We all have many of the same desires: We want to be able to do what we want to do, when we want to do it–and look and feel good along the way. Most want to be self-sufficient and have enough money to be comfortable. We want to be healthy and fit so there are fewer constraints and obstacles in our paths. We want to feel good about how our lives are progressing as well as what we have accomplished so far. We also want to be attractive enough to garner the considerations we desire from others. As shallow and simplistic as all this may sound, it is an honest summation of the human condition.

It is important to be able to care for ourselves, care for those close to us, and enjoy our future. These desires come in many different forms, but the goals mainly involve achieving financial security, maintaining a healthy lifestyle, incorporating purposeful living, and working positively on how we feel about ourselves. Seen through this lens, the same concerns we have for the *future* are concerns we have for *today*. The major difference is that we have more time now to make adjustments to affect the next phases of life. Making incremental changes now can positively impact outcomes in many areas, allowing a person to have a more fruitful life overall.

We could also do the opposite. We could ignore or downplay our future by totally focusing on today. Unfortunately, this is often justified by excuses such as:

- "I have plenty of time."
- "I don't have enough time."
- "I won't live that long anyway."
- "Someone else will take care of it."
- "The government will support me."
- "I can't even make ends meet today."

These excuses are used constantly–and that is really all they are: *excuses*. They are just a means to avoid the hard work and responsibility–and incredible _opportunity_–to be in the driver's seat of life and its outcomes, enabling greater fulfillment.

So, where do we go from here? You will now want to take the ***Ease into Aging: Definitions for Life Assessment*** located in the Appendix. This will help you to truly and accurately understand what you believe about varied aspects of life, happiness, and success. Because many people have differing beliefs about what's really important to personal fulfillment, this evaluation will give you a chance to get in touch with your true beliefs, and not be swayed by others' opinions and beliefs. This assessment is meant to be completed over a period of time with plenty of introspection–not all in one sitting.

In the Appendix you will also find the ***Ease into Aging: Strengths and Weaknesses Survey.*** This will help you assess your motivations and challenges, including what helps you perform more effectively and where you struggle in life. As always, trust your instincts and honestly consider any advice you may find relevant.

No one has a crystal ball–life changes, so these goals and plans may evolve over the years based on situations and events experienced on the journey. Be willing to make adjustments as needed, but don't fall under the spell of any of the short-term plans to success. There will always be fads and approaches touted by new experts who come along, but it is important to recognize that you are embarking on a journey that will take time. You must make a plan and stick with it to arrive at the future you envision today.

CHAPTER THREE

THE PLAN OF ATTACK: HOW DO YOU GET THERE?

"It's your road and yours alone. Others may walk it with you, but no one can walk it for you."

–Rumi
13th Century Poet and Philosopher

Without knowing where you want to go, it is very difficult to control the necessary steps needed to get there. Using the information you've gathered already, go to the ***Ease into Aging Goal Setting Checklist,*** also in the Appendix, and use it to actually write down and plan your goals for the important parts of your life. When you complete it, put a copy on your refrigerator door and bathroom mirror so it is constantly within your view. Keep in mind that plans are fluid and will probably need to be adjusted from time to time based on what happens during your journey. These goals will serve as your "Life GPS," recalculating while you are progressing to keep you going in your preferred direction (and get you back on track if you stray). Fortunately, if you already know where you are ultimately headed, you likely have the ability to make any adjustments necessary to arrive at the intended destination.

Part Two is where you'll find over two hundred tips and strategies that are certain to play an important role in your life and the lives of those around you. Remember, the primary purpose of this book is to inform and educate you on the pitfalls and challenges the future may hold; it is essentially a cheat sheet based on what many others have experienced. The secondary purpose is to provide tips and strategies to get you started in the right direction and to give you tools for success. A final benefit of this process is gaining fulfillment and confidence such that you can advise others in your sphere of influence, helping them to add peace and satisfaction to their years as well.

Your job now is to figure out which strategies apply, when to use them, and how to put them into practice. Chances are, you have recently considered some of these strategies and, even if you haven't already put them into practice, you've already realized they could be applicable down the road.

As you read this book, go through the whole list and mark or highlight all strategies that directly apply to you right now and those that you strongly suspect could apply in the future. Then go back through the list and mark those that apply now to your parents, siblings, children, friends, and others you know who are in different chapters of life. This will help you prioritize their usefulness and help determine which you would like to implement sooner as part of your earliest goals.

There are many ways you could approach this planning exercise for future development. Take it seriously, but don't think of it as a "test" you have to get right the first time. As mentioned before, goal setting and creating a structured plan must be thought of as a fluid process, as each plan will likely require some fine tuning over the months and years.

If you break your life down into stages (or years) you can consider setting goals that are applicable by need or priority. Some may find it helpful to use five-year periods or even one-year increments, depending on age, stage in life, and the amount of flux that you are currently experiencing. You may even choose to categorize goals as short-range, medium-range, and long-range based on the practical timing of each expected achievement. Plug each strategy into the stage in which you believe it fits.

As suggested before, don't be hesitant to consult with the trusted advisors you have used over the years. They can give tremendous insight on what to expect. The doctors, financial advisors, spiritual counselors, and others in whom you have confided can give you sound advice based on their experiences with others—as well as their personal knowledge of you.

Again, let it be noted that there are many avenues to success. One needs to be willing to do the research, find what fits his or her style, and mold each approach to customize it. Whatever the final solution, it's always easier to adjust to, or fix, a problem sooner rather than later. Be constantly vigilant, watching for discreet changes as the years progress so the effects of these problems don't sneak up on you. This is true for health-related, financial, relationship-based, and other issues. You may not be able to stop adverse events from occurring, but at least you can minimize their effect if you are alert.

Control of our lives is a universal desire. We must be willing to make good decisions based on credible sources in order to maintain this control. Look at the process of self-improvement as an <u>investment in your future</u>, and you will be pleasantly surprised how simple it is. Life's obstacles will always be there, but when you are prepared and have a plan to deal with them, you can make life the journey you always hoped it could be.

Part Two

LIFE STRATEGIES

"SOMETIMES THE SMALLEST STEP IN THE RIGHT DIRECTION ENDS UP BEING THE BIGGEST STEP OF YOUR LIFE."

–Naeem Calloway,
Founder, *Get Out The Box,* Inc.

The whole idea of making decisions and changes concerning your future can be overwhelming. It doesn't have to be. You are about to be introduced to over two hundred tips and strategies that can simplify your journey into each new phase of life. A number of these strategies can play a role in several different aspects of your everyday experiences, while others will only be applicable to specific parts.

Following these strategies can actually simplify your life. Some will become part of your routine, while others will take concerted effort and planning to implement. Many will have a profound effect on you, while others will fine tune and hone already existing practices. Once you put them into motion, you will be able to make adjustments, molding them to be even more beneficial.

Refer back to the instructions in Chapter Three and remember to enjoy the process while you formulate your plan of attack for self-improvement. As you go through the lists of tips and strategies, you may chuckle at, disagree with, and even deny that some of them are potential game-changers. It is important to remain openminded regarding the possible positive effects of making these changes.

Not every strategy you attempt will be perfect for your personal lifestyle, but keep in mind that messy trials and experiments can become our best teachers. In learning what doesn't work personally, a person is far more able to recognize and select strategies that do.

CHAPTER FOUR

HEALTH STRATEGIES

"Understanding that we are responsible for our own health empowers us to live our lives to the fullest."

—Anonymous

Many people experience health challenges that consume their life focus, at least for a period of time. We all know someone who is suffering with a health issue that has caused them to make major lifestyle adjustments. Whether it be cancer, recovery from an accident, diabetes, or any number of health concerns, we know that, without overcoming those challenges, the energy they steal away can be further debilitating. Sometimes just the smallest health problem can create embarrassment, cause withdrawal from friends and loved ones, and even lead to more issues that create a downward spiral.

Many health issues can be avoided, or at least delayed or minimized, by taking some small steps early on to make sure they don't become a major factor. It is important to be attuned to any changes in your health and listen to what your body is telling you. Taking proactive, early steps to ensure problems do not occur in the first place is the very best strategy.

Below are some popular strategies and practices for general health and wellbeing. Some may require major adjustments in lifestyle, while others are easily incorporated into an everyday routine. Still others can just be adapted to fine tune an already healthy approach.

As always, it is essential to consult a trusted medical advisor prior to putting any health-related strategy into practice. While this list may contain some of the best practices cited in today's literature, not all strategies are ideal or safe for all individuals, particularly those with pre-existing conditions and those using specific medications.

1. Improve Your Balance and Equilibrium.

Many people suffer terrible, life-altering injuries that could have been avoided if they had maintained adequate balance. Even from an early age, people have falls that cause broken bones, head injuries, and lacerations. As a person gets older, the healing process takes longer, and a fall is far more likely to leave long-term side effects. For example, a childhood broken bone is often entirely forgotten in adulthood, but a person who breaks his or her wrist at 60 may experience pain and limited function indefinitely. We constantly hear about senior citizens who have fallen, broken a hip, torn a knee, or broken other major bones, and have never fully recovered.

Here are some great tips to improve balance:

1. Walk with your head up and your eyes toward where you are going.

2. Learn your *balance point.* This refers to the standing (balance) point where you feel secure and are not rocking. It is usually located just in front of your heel. When you are standing on one or two feet, and you feel the ball of the foot and the heel equally at the same time, you have found it.

3. Use a balance ball to improve balance in a safe environment. While standing on a balance ball, rock side to side and front to back. Do this with your eyes open and closed.

    (Author's note: Balance balls are available at most sporting goods and retail stores and are available for use at most gyms.)

4. Strengthen your legs and keep them strong by doing squatting and lunging exercises on a consistent basis. These can be as simple as sitting slowly onto a chair and getting up without using arm strength to assist (but to guide), if you feel unsteady.

5. Strengthen your core muscles: back muscles, abdominals, and obliques (i.e., the torso). This can be done with stretching, yoga, Pilates, or swimming.

6. Practice Tai Chi, Pilates, or yoga for a full body workout.

2. Drink Enough Water.

Water is important for a multitude of bodily functions. Interestingly enough, many health problems can be traced to an underconsumption of water. Most people do not drink enough water. This is easily understood as there are so many opinions about how much one should consume. These are based on a person's activity level, his or her body style, what medications the person takes, and a host of other factors. If a person's urine is dark yellow, he or she is probably dehydrated. If the person recently ate and stills feel hungry, he or she is probably dehydrated. If an individual feel thirsty, often it is actually dehydration that is the issue. If a person feels listless and lacks energy, it could also be dehydration. Having a dry or sticky mouth, headaches, cracked skin or lips, muscle cramps, or constipation can all be signs of dehydration. Keep in mind that, just as each person's taste for salt and spice in food are different, each person's body is different in how much water is needed for a given day.

Here are some common-sense tips and guidelines to make sure you consume enough water:

1. Consider using the 8 x 8 rule: eight eight-ounce glasses of water spread out through the day. This is the minimum one should drink.

2. If you are physically active, you need to drink more.

3. Avoid consuming foods and liquids that are diuretic in nature (e.g., caffeine and alcohol).

4. If you live in a hot climate, you need to increase your water consumption.

5. About 80 percent of water intake should come from actual water, while approximately 20 percent can come from other foods and drinks (e.g., juice, broth, or tea).

6. It is a good idea to keep a glass or bottle near you so you can drink water throughout the day. This also helps to curb your appetite.

3. Prevent Dripping After Urination.

Besides being embarrassing, post-void dripping could be a sign of some possible health issues. Normally it's just a functional problem brought on by weak muscles, but it could be a symptom of prostatitis, urethral diverticulum, diabetes, or certain neurological disorders. It usually happens when a (hopefully) small amount of urine stays in the urethra after urination.

Here are some tips for what to do if this occurs:

1. Using your fingers, put pressure on the perineum (the area between the anus and scrotum (male) or the vulva (female)), and hold for three seconds. Perform this a couple times just after urinating.

2. Wear dark colored pants to prevent embarrassing moments.

3. Consider wearing a panty liner (women).

4. Research, learn, and practice Kegel exercises.

5. Ask a doctor about pelvic floor therapy, as this can be very beneficial in retraining muscles for women who have endured several pregnancies, as well as men with bladder or bowel dysfunction.

6. See a urologist if the problem persists.

4. Learn to Cook.

Preparing your own meals has so many advantages. You will obviously eat more healthy choices, you will save a lot of money in comparison to eating out, and you can even develop thinking and processing skills important to maintaining strong mental acuity. Cooking can allow you to create gifts and care packages for others, and preparing food can itself be a social activity and an important part of interacting with friends and loved ones.

In terms of the health benefits, when you prepare your own meals, you know exactly what's going in them. You can monitor the intake of contents such as bad fats, MSG, and sodium, which are detrimental to health and found in abundance in most restaurant meals. You can also monitor the amount of food you consume more easily when you prepare your own meals.

Here are some thoughts on getting started:

1. Learn the various measuring terms.

2. Keep a good set of sharp knives.

3. Learn grilling skills. Start with a simple kitchen grill and, if or when you're ready, move up to a top-of-the-line model.

4. Start with simple recipes and gradually work up to more complicated meals.

5. Take advantage of the many cooking programs available, or watch (and re-watch) internet videos with techniques that you wish to try.

6. Seek advice from others who are more advanced in the art of preparing meals.

7. Invite friends over to share a kitchen and cook together, making it a social event.

8. Take a cooking class with friends in lieu of meeting up to go out to eat.

5. Skip the After-Dinner Cocktail and Take a 20-30 Minute After-Dinner Walk.

"Walking off your dinner" is such a great idea. Chances are you won't break any speed records, but that's not the point. Cutting back on alcohol consumption is always a good idea, but actually getting away from the dinner table–getting out of the house and getting a little exercise–helps with digestion and lowering blood-sugar levels after a meal. Your walk doesn't need to be brisk. It could and should just be a stroll. It can help you relax, think about the day, or spend some time with your spouse or family. It may also have a few social benefits–you may even get to know your neighbors better.

6. Only Floss the Teeth You Wish to Keep.

Inadequate dental care can cause many health issues. We all know how important it is to brush our teeth, but dental care is so much more. We need to make sure we are consistently taking care of not only our teeth, but also our gums. Many other health issues manifest in the mouth. Certain diseases can actually be detected through a dental exam, such as diabetes, anemia, and some cancers. In fact, according to the American Academy of General Dentistry (2011), 90 percent of common medical ailments have oral symptoms. So, if you have any problems with your teeth, mouth, breath, or gums, don't hesitate to have these checked out by a medical professional.

Here are some things that need to be done on a regular basis to ensure one's mouth remains healthy:

1. Brush at least two times a day. It's a good idea to rotate between an electric toothbrush and a manual brush to ensure better coverage.

2. Floss at least once a day. Be careful not to cut your gums–the idea is to be thorough, but not aggressive. It is a good idea to rotate among different styles of floss so as not to irritate your gums.

3. Have your teeth cleaned twice a year under normal circumstances, and more often if there are issues. X-rays

usually only need to be done every couple of years (unless the dental professional notices something serious).

4. Visit your dentist at least once a year. This visit can be combined with a cleaning appointment.

5. Quit smoking, chewing tobacco, and the use of all other tobacco products.

6. Use a mouthwash or rinse that fights plaque and other oral problems.

7. If you tend to have canker sores, use a medication or supplement that is designed to at least lessen their effect on the gums, cheeks, and lips.

7. Try These Things to Improve Your Sleep Quality.

We've all heard how important sleep is to overall health, and the facts don't lie. People with sleep issues seem to have other health problems as well, including increased risk of heart disease and obesity. It can be confusing to determine how much sleep we actually need, and it is true that some people need more than others. The amount of sleep a person needs even varies during different times of life.

Many find consistent deep sleep elusive for a variety of reasons including worry, pain, and worn-out bedding, but here are some strategies for a great night's sleep:

1. Take the TV out of the bedroom.

2. Make sure the bedroom is as dark as a cave, and also as quiet.

3. Leave your phone in another room unless you are anticipating an important call (at least keep the phone on silent mode).

4. Stop all computer, phone, and TV usage at least an hour before you turn in for the night.

5. Take a hot shower or bath right before going to bed.

6. Do not consume caffeine within two to three hours of bedtime.

7. Learn your best sleeping position. It may vary throughout the night.

8. Deal with any challenges you had during the day and "put these to rest" before turning in for the evening.

9. Read something spiritual or uplifting right before turning off the light.

10. Do not wear a smartwatch to bed. The light will interrupt your sleep. *(Author's note: I know of people, myself included, who have awoken the next morning feeling energized, but their smartwatches told them they had a bad night's sleep!)*

11. Skip taking a nap during the day if you are not sleeping well at night.

12. Make sure your sheets are 100 percent cotton. Many stylish-looking bed linens are polyester or polyester blends, and these do not breathe, causing night sweats or skin irritation.

13. After sex is a great time to relax and sleep!

Bottom line: Most people need between six and nine hours of sleep per night. With practice, you will know how much is best for you. Sleep needs vary during different periods of our lives and there are many variables to consider. If a person is waking up at approximately the same time every morning without an alarm, he or she is probably getting the amount needed for that given point in life.

8. While Watching TV...

It's been said that ***sitting is the new smoking*** in terms of its adverse effects on health. Unfortunately, when we watch television, we are usually sitting. Television is such a part of our lives. We actually spend more time in front of it than we realize. Before we know it, we've been sitting for two or three hours. When we combine this with the time spent at a desk or table working, eating, and socializing, as well as driving, that's an awfully long time to be stationary!

Here are some strategies to lessen the impact sitting has on your health:

1. 1. Time and record how much time you actually spend sitting over a period of two or three days. It will astound you. Then determine how much of this time is spent sitting in front of a TV.

2. Sit with your feet flat on the floor and don't cross your legs. Try to sit up straight and practice good posture while viewing the television. Have the TV far enough away that you aren't squinting and straining your eyes.

3. Try to relax while viewing. Tensing the shoulders and back over a period of time can cause issues.

4. Get up and walk around during each commercial break.

5. Have the TV just loud enough so that you can hear it, rather than blaring.

6. Use the time while watching to do some stretching exercises.

7. Rotate sitting and standing between commercial breaks.

8. Keep a hand-strengthening device nearby and use it while watching.

9. Consider watching TV while walking on a treadmill or using a stationary bike, if these are available to you.

9. Ask a Doctor if these Supplements Could Benefit You.

It is difficult to turn on the TV or go on social media and not see advertisements touting the benefits of supplements–those to take with meals, enhance sexual performance, build muscle, or increase your lifespan. Supplements are touted as if they will magically change your life!

Most health-conscious people believe in taking supplements, but it is important to do the research first, and then consult with a trusted medical advisor to see what might be beneficial given a person's unique health situation before attempting to add a supplement into the daily regimen.

Check out these supplements:

SUPPLEMENT	BEST SOURCE	EVIDENCED-BASED BENEFITS
Resveratrol	red wine, capsules	anti-aging, skin health, antioxidant
Calcium	dairy	bone health (take only if needed)
Multi-vitamin	capsules	easy source of many supplements
CoQ10	capsule	heart health, antioxidant
Fish oil	fish, capsules	heart health, inflammation fighter, weight control
Niacin	meat, capsule	lower cholesterol and triglycerides

Turmeric	capsule	inflammation fighter, pain, possible cancer prevention
Lysine	capsule	cure and prevention of canker sores
Probiotic	Greek yogurt, capsule	gut health, heart health, weight control, bowel difficulties
Magnesium	diet, capsule	energy boost, diabetes aid, migraines
Tart Cherry	cherries, capsule	energy boost, brain health, recovery, memory
Potassium	fruits and veggies	fluid balance, kidney stones
Vitamin D	fish, sun, supplement	various body functions attributed to age or lack of sun/exposure

There are many other supplements available that may be beneficial for specific needs. But, when it comes to taking any supplement, it is vital to first confer with a trusted medical advisor, as some can interact with medications or worsen certain health conditions. As with all advice, it is important to understand the benefits and drawbacks and continually monitor the effects. Keep in mind that most vitamins and minerals are available in food sources, so eating fruits and vegetables (for example) is almost always a better option than supplements. In some cases, however, it may be difficult to measure the amount of a given substance being consumed if a person is attempting to address a known deficiency. A qualified medical professional can and should assist with this.

10. Recognize that Most Back Problems Come from the Front.

This is a bit of an exaggeration. The point is, it is necessary to keep your abdominals, obliques, and chest muscles, strong to help support your back when it is under stress. Stretching, good posture, and avoidance of sitting for too long can do a tremendous amount to decrease back pain. It can also help to lose a bit of weight (if necessary), as extra around the middle can change the center of gravity and a person's gait, contributing to discomfort.

If you are dealing with back pain, do the research, consult with a professional trainer, and start working on a solution. When in doubt, a few sessions of physical therapy–or getting involved in yoga, Tai Chi, or Pilates–can get a person started off on the right track. If the problems persist and cause you to make adjustments to your lifestyle, don't hesitate to make an appointment with your trusted medical advisor.

11. Consider Fasting.

Many people fast, either for health or religious reasons. If it is something you want to do–for any reason–here are some different ways that people use fasting to increase health:

1. One type of intermittent fasting is called the 16/8 plan, where individuals only consume food during an eight-hour window during each day.

2. Another type of intermittent fasting involves restricting food intake for one or two days a week (i.e., women consume 500 calories per day and men consume 600 calories) and eating normally on non-fasting days.

3. One popular version involves fasting for a 12- to 24-hour window (or longer) on a few days per week.

Most of the above plans also advise against eating after dinner or into the later evening hours, and they emphasize a reduction in the carbohydrate and sugar intake overall. Whatever plan fits your lifestyle, a person should always contact a medical professional before changing his or her diet. It is common to experience some side effects when first starting a fasting program; these include malaise, fainting, mood swings, dehydration, constipation, and lack of energy, among others, but these generally fade within the first few days of beginning a program. Some people also find it beneficial to work themselves toward longer fasts by beginning a fast after dinner, sleeping through most of it, then skipping breakfast and eating an early lunch.

Fasting is one of the most popular health and fitness trends and has been closely studied over the last few years. This is a great way to lose weight if you choose, increase energy, improve your overall health and simplify your lifestyle. Dr. Jason Fung, author of *The Obesity Code* and *The Complete Guide to Fasting,* and a leading expert in therapeutic fasting, states that, in conjunction with oversight by a medical doctor, these methods can be used to lose weight, reduce hypertension, and reestablish healthy blood glucose levels (Fung, 2016).

For whatever reason you wish to fast, don't jump into it. This new way of life should be eased into over a period of time so that your body can adjust. Prolonged fasting can cause serious health problems that need to be considered when making this decision, and any person who is using medication will require a doctor's oversight to ensure safety along the way.

12. Wash Your Hands!

The importance of washing hands cannot be overstated. In this day and age of new viruses and diseases, we cannot be too careful about spreading and contracting all kinds of health problems. The experts tell us repeatedly that the first line of defense is to clean and sanitize hands–and to do so often. There are many portable, pocket-sized hand-sanitizing products readily available for this purpose, and if used often and correctly, these can help to reduce the chances of becoming sick. It is a good idea to find products that are effective against bacteria *and* viruses, but soap and water are the very best defenses.

13. Be Cautious with Caffeine.

A few years ago, if an Olympic athlete had over 12 micrograms of caffeine per milliliter in his urine and won an Olympic medal, he (or she) would be forced to forfeit it. That is the equivalent of about 8 espressos over the course of just a few hours! The International Olympic Committee has adjusted the restrictions on caffeine, but the jury is still out on how much caffeine a person can and should consume with regard to safety.

Most of us are not Olympic athletes, but it is still good to know how much caffeine is appropriate, as it is contained in so many foods and drinks. How much is too much? That is a relative question. A small cup of breakfast blend coffee has about 100 mg of caffeine. While sources such as the Mayo Clinic (2020) state that it is safe to consume up to 400 mg per day, that may not be advisable or entirely "moderate" for every person. It is widely believed that a moderate amount of caffeine is good for most people, but too much can cause sleeplessness, jitters, and heart palpitations. Here are some effective guidelines to use with caffeine:

1. Know how much you are consuming.

2. Be aware of the different sources, as they may surprise you.

3. Do not consume caffeine within three hours of bedtime if you find it affects your sleep.

4. Do not consume large amounts of caffeine on an empty stomach.

5. Restrict the consumption of caffeinated products such as sodas and energy drinks. Many of the other ingredients in these items are not beneficial.

6. Balance a caffeinated drink with the same amount of water.

7. Restrict caffeine consumption in young children.

14. Allow Yourself Time to Recover from Injury or Illness.

Recovering from injury or illness can really throw your life out of sync. Here are some tips to lessen the impact:

1. **Make your recovery paramount. Following your trusted medical advisor's advice is the best way to bounce back.**

2. Attempt to continue your daily routine to the degree possible.

3. Keep your body as mobile as possible—you may have to be creative.

4. Adjust your diet. If you are inactive and continue your present diet, you will probably gain unwanted weight.

5. Keep your mind active and stay engaged socially, if at all possible.

15. Do These Things When Eating Out.

Eating out is one of life's great pleasures. Whether it's for business, as a social activity, or just a lack of desire to prepare meals, many people find themselves spending a lot of time eating foods they normally try to (and should) avoid. Here are some approaches to keeping it healthy when dining out:

1. Eat at establishments with healthy options on the menu.
2. Say "no" to the appetizer or use an appetizer as your entree.
3. Ask for the dressing on the side when ordering a salad.
4. Hide the bread basket.
5. Restrict alcohol consumption during meals. Alcohol enhances your appetite.
6. Ask the server to bring a take-home container with the meal and divide it *before* you start eating.
7. Remind yourself to eat slowly. You won't eat as much.
8. Split a meal with a fellow diner.
9. Forego dessert except on special occasions; then, get one with enough forks for all to share one item.
10. Don't be afraid to leave food at the table. It's better to waste it than to overeat.

16. Take A Short Nap.

According to research done by Catherine E. Milner and Kimberly Cote for the *Journal of Sleep Research* (2009), taking a short nap has been shown to be a great strategy to improve health and increase productivity. Here are some ways to incorporate a nap into your daily routine to enhance well-being and performance:

1. Try to nap in the same location and approximately at the same time.
2. Don't focus on trying to sleep–focus on trying to relax.
3. Keep it around 20-30 minutes.
4. Clear your mind of today's concerns.
5. Turn off your phone.
6. When finished, move around and rehydrate.
7. As mentioned before, if napping interferes with your nightly sleep pattern, consider deleting it from your day.

17. Decrease Pain and Soreness.

In addition to stretching, yoga, Pilates, and Tai Chi, a simple hand-held massager is a fantastic tool to relieve everyday aches and pains. Try to use one that has a multitude of massage heads and adjustable speeds, as they come in all different sizes, shapes, and prices. Experiment and you will see the benefits quickly. If pain persists or seems to intensify, don't hesitate to set up an appointment with your trusted medical advisor.

18. Protect Your Skin.

This advice cannot be overstated, and it means more than just wearing sunscreen. It is important to apply these guidelines, so that your skin doesn't become a major health issue down the road:

1. Always use SPF 30 sunscreen (or higher) during sun exposure and reapply often. Apply extra to the forearms, face, and neck.
2. Watch the time of exposure and the sun intensity to avoid sunburns.
3. Use sunscreen-infused lip balm.
4. Bathe or shower in lukewarm, not hot, water.
5. Use skin cleansers instead of harsh soaps.
6. Apply moisturizing cream after showering while the skin is still damp. Don't skimp and focus on trouble areas that are overly dry.
7. Don't use moisturizers on the face that are designed for the body.
8. Use a silk pillow cover when sleeping.
9. See a dermatologist at least once a year (or more often if you have any skin problems).

19. Have Your Eyes and Ears Checked at Least Yearly.

It can be difficult to manage daily activities with a major hearing loss or loss of vision. Because the loss of the senses is usually progressive and slow, many people endure years with a deficit that, if they had been examined regularly, could have been mitigated or minimized before serious deficiency was permanent. As age increases, both vision and hearing have a tendency to get worse. Fortunately, they don't usually fail quickly, so there is usually time to address (and often remedy) issues as long as a person is being checked regularly.

20. Try an Inversion Table.

An inversion table is one of the most under-utilized and beneficial health devices available today. Using one regularly helps to keep the spine aligned, slow down body shrinkage due to aging, and alleviate many aches and pains. Keep these tips in mind when purchasing and using this great health aid:

1. Do the research before you buy a table and try different devices.

2. Discuss the use of an inversion table with a trusted healthcare advisor before trying one or making a purchase (especially if you have hypertension or a pre-existing back condition).

3. Check with your eyecare specialist before using this device if you have eye-pressure problems.

4. Start slowly and work up to about 10-15 minutes a day of use. You don't have to go 180 degrees (i.e., fully inverted) for it to be effective.

5. Use it as a meditation and relaxation tool.

21. Be Skeptical of Advertisements.

Be leery of ALL advertisements for products touting health benefits. As previously mentioned, we are flooded with ads for products that are touted as having "amazing effects on health and well-being." When considering using something new for health reasons, apply these principles:

1. Have an open mind, but also a healthy dose of skepticism.

2. Consult your trusted health advisor beforehand to ensure there are no possible adverse reactions related to your personal physiology.

3. Do your own research.

4. Discuss the item with those who have actually used the product you are considering.

5. Start slow and monitor the effects.

6. Don't start using a number of new products at the same time. They may have unhealthy interactions. You also may not be able to discern which is beneficial.

22. Choose the Right Shoes.

Many physical problems can be linked to issues with the feet and can be caused by wearing the wrong shoes. Hip, back, and leg problems are often caused by wearing ill-fitting footwear. Fortunately, they can also be corrected, or at least minimized, by selecting appropriate options. Style is important but should not be the main reason for choosing footwear. Here are some tips for choosing and wearing one of the most important articles of your wardrobe:

1. Don't depend on a typical retailer to tell you what size you wear. Most true orthopedic shoe stores evaluate your feet for the correct sizing.

2. Know if you wear a narrow, medium, or wide shoe, not just the numerical size.

3. Don't buy shoes without trying them on and walking in them. Chances are, if they are uncomfortable when you try them on, they will probably remain that way.

4. Purchase shoes for the activity for which they are specifically designed.

5. If you have a pronation or supination problem, wear shoes that correct these structural challenges.

6. Wear shoes that are cushioned and have arch support.

7. Save the flip flops for around the house. Or better yet, don't even wear them.

8. Tie the laces snug, but not too tight.

9. Wear shoes around the house if you have hard floors.

(Author's Note: High heels? Wear at your own peril.)

23. Try These Tips if Pooping is a Problem.

We've all been there. Sometimes we're constipated; other times we have diarrhea. Either can cause discomfort, but they can also be signs of poor diet choices and even more serious health problems. Surprisingly, the solutions for both are usually similar. Either could be caused by medications, certain supplements, travel, Irritable Bowel Syndrome, poor hydration, too little fiber, too much caffeine, menstruation, or stress. Sometimes it is just a low-level sensitivity to a particular food item, such as nuts or dairy. Discovering the cause enables a person to find the cure. When dealing with bowel problems consider these guidelines:

1. Increase intake of water throughout the day.

2. Drink warm liquids that are not diuretic in nature.

3. Add more fiber to the diet by eating more fruits and vegetables.

4. Keep a food diary to monitor food intake to discern a possible problem or sensitivity.

5. Use a Squatty Potty.™ Correct use of a positioning device changes the sitting angle on the toilet, opening

up the bend in the distal colon, making it easier to poop.

6. Be hesitant to take any medication or over-the-counter drug

7. for these types of problems. They can be habit forming and should only be used as a last resort.

8. Increase your daily exercise and activity level.

9. Do not resist the urge: When you have to go…go!

24. Dump All Tobacco Products.

Anyone considering the use of tobacco products, at any time, is making a serious mistake. If you don't use them, don't ever start. If you do use them, do whatever it takes to stop. There is no justification for the risk to health and the damage it does to the body.

25. Donate Blood.

Donating blood is good for so many reasons. It is also a simple process that usually only takes about an hour. These are just a few of the benefits of donating regularly:

1. Receiving the satisfaction of helping out at least two to three other people with the gift of life.

2. Obtaining a "mini physical" each time you donate.

3. Knowing that the blood bank will notify you if your blood shows any health abnormalities, helping you keep abreast of any potential issues.

4. Donating blood burns approximately the same number of calories as burned during a one-hour intense cardio workout.

5. Reducing the potential storage of too much iron in your system. *(Author's note: Excess iron can make people feel tired, sick, and nauseous, or lead to liver and joint damage, among other problems.)*

6. Inducing the body to produce more healthy red blood cells. Giving up some of your older cells triggers the body to churn out fresh cells. Many people report feeling increased energy and productivity within a few weeks of giving blood, as about one-tenth of the blood cells are brand new and at peak performance.

As always, it is important to consult with your trusted medical advisor before starting to give blood. There are a number of ways to donate, so make sure you use a reputable blood bank and always ask what they do with the blood donations they obtain.

26. Treat Bad Breath.

Bad breath, or halitosis, is embarrassing! And many times, we don't even know we have it. Even more important, this can be a sign of issues in your mouth or digestive tract.

If someone you know is brave enough to tell you that your breath stinks, take the following steps:

1. Drink a sufficient amount of water. Most of the time this will curb it.

2. Brush your teeth often. When doing so, also brush your tongue and your gums. Consider using a tongue scraper at the same time you brush.

3. Use mouthwash, gum, or mints when you can.

4. If you are on a high-protein diet, use extra precautions, as this can be a major cause of halitosis.

5. Quit using tobacco products.

6. Visit a dentist to check for signs of tooth decay and gum disease.

If the problem persists, it is important to make sure your trusted medical advisor is aware. If there is a chronic problem— he or she may have already noticed!

27. Deal with Anger Properly.

Many, if not most of us, have been conditioned to deal with anger in one of two ways: either bottle it up or let it rip.

Unfortunately, both of these can be dangerous from a health standpoint.

Studies indicate that people who consistently suppress their anger tend to live shorter lives and are more apt to die early from diseases such as cancer and heart failure (Davison & Mostofsky, 2010; Enright, 2017). The Mayo Clinic (2020) explains that anger releases stress hormones such as cortisol and adrenaline, which also make a person prone to developing depression, hypertension, stroke, diabetes, and peptic ulcers, as well as other stress-related health conditions. Additionally, people who scream and holler when they are angry, trying to get it out of their systems, run other health risks such as increased blood pressure and elevated heart rate. This puts stress on the cardiovascular system, making individuals more as likely to have a heart attack (Davison & Mostofsky, 2010; Mayo Clinic, 2020).

So, what is one to do? Below are some strategies that can help you avoid the dangers of anger:

1. Know and avoid the people, things, and situations that trigger anger.

2. Talk about how you feel to someone. If you talk to the person who causes the anger, discuss the situation calmly and rationally. Attack the situation, not the person, and avoid putting the individual on the defensive. Discussion and resolution can be very cathartic.

3. Pledge to yourself that you will avoid any spontaneous reactions to any stressful situations. Take a break and walk away to cool down for at least 10 minutes before reacting.

4. Deeply inhale and exhale slowly at least 10 times when you feel anger coming on.

5. Exercise regularly to help release frustration. The Mayo Clinic (2020) article, "Exercise and Stress: Get Moving to Manage Stress," states that being physically active is an excellent strategy to manage anger, reduce the influence of stress-based hormones, and increase the production of endorphins (happy neurotransmitters) by the brain.

6. Drop your voice to a lower and quieter tone if tempers flare. This can diffuse tense situations.

7. Keep your ego under control by remembering the costs to relationships and your reputation when melting down in front of others.

Anger has ruined many relationships and caused many business failings. Chances are, if you learn to control it, your life will be more comfortable, and you will probably live longer.

28. Improve your Flexibility.

Flexibility in the body and joints should be a major concern to everyone, as it allows for better balance, less joint pain, and longevity with respect to retaining the ability to do the activities we enjoy. It's pretty obvious who is flexible and who isn't. Unfortunately, it requires ongoing attention, or you lose it. Increasing flexibility:

1. Reduces the risk of injury.

2. Helps to relieve post-exercise soreness.

3. Improves posture.

4. Helps to manage stress.

5. Enhances relaxation.

6. Improves functional fitness.

7. Promotes good circulation.

8. Helps in preparation for exercise.

9. Decreases the risk of lower back pain.

There is a lot of information available regarding the benefits of flexibility. The best approach is to spend some face-to-face time with a professional certified in flexibility training, but simply starting with yoga, Tai Chi, or a beginner Pilates class (or video) can also get a person started, as the goal is increasing range of motion and activity gradually. There are also many articles and videos available from a variety of different sources, allowing for a customized approach.

29. Sleep with a Weighted Blanket.

Many sources such as Healthline.com extoll the benefits of sleeping with a weighted blanket. Weighted blankets were originally designed for those with autism, to help them sleep better and deal with anxiety. In recent years, they have found their way into mainstream usage for the same reasons and have proven effective. They have also been touted as a great tool for teenagers and adults who have been diagnosed with ADHD (Lockett, 2019).

When considering a heavy blanket, a consumer should recognize:

1. They can be expensive, but they are well worth the investment.

2. They are usually filled with either plastic or glass pellets that make them heavy (either option works).

3. They typically range from five to 25 pounds. A general rule of thumb is to use a blanket that is 10 percent of the person's bodyweight. For example, if a man weighs approximately 200 pounds, he should use a 20-pound blanket.

4. These should NEVER be used with young children.

(Author's Note: Weighted blankets are not for everyone, but they are worth considering for those who have sleep difficulties or anxiety issues.)

30. Improve Your Sex Life.

Studies done by several health organizations have attributed numerous physical and emotional benefits to having a satisfying, healthy sex life. An analysis of these studies, published in the *Journal of Social and Behavioral Studies* (2016), indicates that a good sex life improves fitness, reduces pain, improves immune function and increases heart health. Emotionally it helps to boost self-esteem, enhance levels of happiness, improve intimacy and commitment, and relieve stress (Liu, Waite, and Shen, 2016).

Sian Ferguson states in her article, *"Is Sex Important in a Relationship? 12 Things to Consider"* (2019), that because there are so many feelings and beliefs about sex–and different approaches- no approach is wrong as long as all involved are on board with it.

It is important to note, however, that a good sex life can and should be an integral part of a couple's fulfillment within a relationship, regardless of age. Use it or lose it!

> *(Author's note: Your sex life is your business. There are many moral and religious considerations attached to the subject of sex. Because of this, I have chosen not to present or discuss any specific techniques or practices that involve sex.)*

31. Learn How to Relax.

We all know how to relax–or do we? There are so many relaxation techniques being touted and they all probably work for some people, but this is a very individualized subject. Relaxation is hard to define because it means many things to many different people. For some it may mean communing with nature, exercising, doing a favored hobby, using meditation or yoga, or spending time with friends and family. Relaxation is part of the essential "me time" that is necessary to living well.

It is important to determine what relaxation means to you personally, so you can then find the ability to relax much easier. Experiment with different activities and techniques to discover what works. The proof is how you feel during and after you begin working on this aspect of life.

32. Know Your Numbers.

Tracking different aspects of your health is very important and also relatively easy. There are many tests available through your trusted medical advisor, and also through phone apps and tools available at your local pharmacy.

Here is a list of health-related variables that should be measured at least on a yearly basis (or more often depending on your health status):

1. Blood Pressure (BP). High blood pressure (or hypertension) is often called the "silent killer." This can be measured and monitored at practically any drug store

or pharmacy. Inexpensive blood pressure cuffs are also available for home use and monitoring.

2. Fasting Blood Sugar (FBS). This test is usually done as part of a physical by a trusted medical advisor. It shows if a person is considered diabetic (or headed in that direction).

3. Resting Heart Rate (RHR). This should be taken while in a restful state. It can be done by the individual very easily. It shows the presence (or possibility) of many heart problems. Most blood pressure cuffs also measure the heart rate while testing.

4. Cholesterol. This measure indicates two types of cholesterol that are found in the blood. It is usually expressed in three numbers; "good cholesterol" (HDL, or high-density lipoprotein), "bad cholesterol" (LDL, or low-density lipoprotein), and total. Cholesterol is a necessary component of cells, but having too much of the "bad" type can be an indicator that heart disease and atherosclerosis may develop. Many doctors also look at the ratio between the good and bad forms of cholesterol.

5. Triglycerides. Triglycerides are the main constituents of body fat and are also located in the bloodstream. While these are absolutely necessary for life function, high triglyceride counts indicate a major risk for coronary disease, even more so than high LDL values.

6. Body Mass Index (BMI). A person's BMI is a ratio between his or her height and weight. This metric is used by many doctors to assess risk for adverse health complications. While important, it should only be considered in combination with other factors such as obesity, diabetes, and high blood pressure. A person who has a slightly higher than ideal BMI can be very healthy and fit, and may even be *more so* than a person with a low-normal BMI, based on activity level, muscle density, and diet. Muscle weighs more than fat, so many athletic or muscular men, for example, have slightly elevated BMI values but are still very healthy.

7. Bone Mineral Density (BMD). A BMD compares an individual's bone density (or mass) to that of a healthy person. It is the best way to measure bone strength. Low scores can indicate the onset or presence of osteoporosis.

8. Vision. One's vision usually weakens slowly, so an annual (at least) vision screening is necessity at any age. This can also allow for early detection of conditions for which there are therapeutic treatments such as cataracts, macular degeneration, and glaucoma.

9. Prostate Specific Antigen (PSA). The PSA test is imperative for men over the age of 40 (or earlier if the person has a family history of prostate cancer or enlarged prostate (BPH)).

(Author's note: Prostate cancer is becoming more prevalent in men under 40, even those with no family history.)

10. C-Reactive Protein (CRP). The C-Reactive Protein test is one of the most effective indicators of inflammation and is considered one of the most accurate markers for heart disease. It does have a tendency to be general in nature, so further testing is needed to confirm any suspicions that a trusted medical advisor may have. For example, a high CRP might be an indication that a person is simply recovering from illness, but it could also be an indication of an underlying inflammatory or autoimmune condition.

It is important to take advantage of the many health screenings received during an annual physical. Your trusted medical advisor can help guide you, but don't rely solely on his or her judgment. It is appropriate to advocate on your own behalf and ask questions if you have a concern about your health.

33. Practice Falling.

Every year people of all ages die or are seriously injured from falls. With the knowledge of how to fall, many injuries can be avoided–or at least minimized.

Repetition can aid in muscle memory, allowing you to react properly if you ever find yourself actually falling. It can be comforting to know that you are better prepared to protect yourself. If you feel comfortable doing so, locate a place, like a soft grassy area, to practice using these tried and true falling techniques.

1. Protect your head. Tuck your chin and put your hands and arms in front of your face if falling forward.

2. Turn to your side when you fall.

3. Keep your arms and legs bent.

4. Try to relax when you start to fall, rather than stiffening or trying to flail and fight it.

5. If you can, roll out.

6. Spread out the force of the fall throughout your body.

   (Author's Note: Improving your balance and equilibrium, using the techniques stated earlier in this chapter, can help to avoid falls.)

34. Know the Signs of a Stroke: F.A.S.T.

The effects of a stroke can be limited if the person receives care quickly. If you recognize these simple signs, which are abbreviated in the easy-to-remember acronym F.A.S.T., you could help prevent serious injury or death:

1. FACE DROOPING. Try to smile: An irregular expression is an obvious sign of a stroke.

2. <u>A</u>RM WEAKNESS. Try to raise your arms over your head. If it's a struggle, get help immediately.

3. <u>S</u>PEECH. Read a simple sentence out loud–or repeat a phrase back to someone. If it's slurred, garbled, or hard to understand, get to a hospital.

4. <u>T</u>IME TO CALL 911. If any of the above symptoms occur, it is important to quickly get medical attention, as a stroke is a true medical emergency.

It can be difficult to diagnose a stroke. If you think you may be having one, try to find someone to put you through these tests. Don't ever drive to get help if you suspect you are having a stroke–call an ambulance. You may not be in any condition to drive, and you could lose consciousness or even enter a state of delirium while driving.

35. Use Alcohol Sensibly.

It is difficult to find a really good reason to drink alcohol. There are some health benefits to alcohol consumption, but they can usually be derived from other sources. Alcohol overuse and abuse has many adverse health effects even beyond those frequently cited.

The effect that alcohol abuse has on an individual, a family, and even whole organizations cannot be overstated. Alcohol should never be used to self-medicate for pain, anxiety, stress, or anger. A representative of Florida's Bay Pines Medical

Center once said to me, 'a great number of hospitals could close their doors permanently if alcohol abuse was not a factor.' That is a succinct way of summing up the conflict.

Bottom line: If you drink alcohol, do so responsibly.

In Conclusion: Be Your Own Health Advocate

No one knows you better than you, and no one cares about you more than you do. It is ultimately up to you to make sure your health is taken care of. Of course, your family and friends want you to be healthy, but they have their own priorities and perspective. A doctor may have your best interest at heart, but, because of patient loads, requirements of suppliers, and possible lack of experience, a doctor can only do so much. While it is absolutely important to benefit from others' experiences and know-how, your health is your responsibility. Build a list of medical advisors you trust and whose perspectives align with yours. You will need them from time to time, but always be in research mode and monitor your health like your life depends on it–because it really does!

CHAPTER FIVE

RELATIONSHIP STRATEGIES

"The biggest cause of joy and happiness in our lives is our relationships: the biggest cause of pain and sorrow in our lives is our relationships."

—Author

Dealing with people can be a big challenge, and we have to navigate this activity all the time! A big part of life includes interaction with others, regardless of what stage we are in or what occupies our time.

It is vital for our well-being to have others involved in our world. A study performed by the National Academies of Sciences, Engineering, and Medicine (2020) indicates that psychological factors such as loneliness, depression, and anxiety are strongly correlated with poor physiological outcomes in those who do not closely and meaningfully interact with others on a regular basis. These psychological factors can contribute to a multitude health conditions, including a 50 percent increase in the risk of developing dementia, 29 percent increase in the risk of heart disease, and 32 percent increase in the risk of stroke.

One of the best ways to guard against this is to develop and nurture healthy relationships; and it is wise to be careful when doing so. People are generally good and want what's best for us, but when meeting new people, we need to slow down and be sure of their character. It is important to truly get to know a person before fully trusting him or her. We also want to make sure we give others a chance to know us better, while not throwing ourselves at them.

Even with cell phones, social media, and relationship gurus available, it is not always easy to truly present an honest version of oneself while interacting with others. People skills are so important, both in familial settings and in the working world. Yet, we often find ourselves coming up short in relationship expectations.

Relationships take on many forms. Some develop into long-term connections, while others are short encounters. Some have a profound effect on our lives, while others just seem to be coincidental. Regardless of their purpose or longevity, it is important to learn how to deal with people in a positive and meaningful way so that you get the most out of what life has to offer.

In this chapter, you will find some excellent strategies to help develop and nurture relationships. These even include ways to deal with toxic relationships and mechanisms to manage individuals who, generally speaking, do not have your best interests at heart.

1. Keep Your Advice to Yourself.

Unless you are specifically asked for advice, don't give it out–even if you are an expert on the subject. And even then, give it sparingly. People usually aren't looking for help when they tell you about a situation or problem they are having. They just want to be heard.

A few reasons to be more forthcoming with advice are:

1. If you are acting in an official instructional or leadership capacity.

2. If you are a counsellor and the person has come to you for counselling.

3. If the person is doing something that is detrimental to himself or herself, or to others.

2. Form and Be a Part of an Accountability Group.

An accountability group is a collection of people, having much in common, who meet regularly to discuss and share each other's lives. The purpose of such a group is for members to gain insight from each other and to offer constructive criticism and encouragement. It is designed to be totally private, and no member shares any information with anyone outside of the group.

Because of the nature of the group, it is vital that members are chosen with great care and all understand and respect its purpose. All members need to be open, have no personal agenda, and honestly believe that privacy is essential for the sake of each member. Really effective accountability groups take a while to come together and can vary in size from just a few members up to a couple dozen participants.

Here are some important things to consider when forming an accountability group:

1. It is a good idea to consider developing the group from a larger group, such as a church organization.

2. The group should meet consistently, but not too often. Once a month is a great interval for gatherings, and meetings should be regularly scheduled to be effective.

3. Except under special situations, it's a good idea not to have two or more members from within one family in the group.

4. Each meeting should have a theme or topic to get it started, but this should not restrict the content of conversations as they flow.

5. Each meeting should begin and end with discussion of the importance and necessity of the privacy requirement.

6. It is a good idea to rotate leadership duties during each meeting.

7. New members can be introduced, but the inclusion of new members must be agreed upon by all other members.

8. Notetaking should be restricted at meetings.

9. The group can be informal as long as all participants understand the purpose and parameters.

10. Many groups are done face to face, but some are available online and through apps. There is a broad array of accountability groups and formats focusing on a variety of topics.

If an accountability group is planned and developed, and it keeps the members' best intentions in the forefront, people's lives can be positively altered for many years to come.

(Author's note: More information regarding how to set up and develop an accountability group is available at: www.habitsforwellbeing.com)

3. Realize You Can't Please Everyone All the Time.

This is one of those cold hard facts that we constantly try to prove wrong. Regardless of who you are and whom you are interacting with, you will never be able to make everyone happy.

What's the best thing to do? Here are some considerations:

1. Don't confuse facts with opinions. If you're not sure, tell others that what is shared is an opinion.

2. Try to present both sides of a situation when appropriate, and make sure people know where you stand.

3.   Learn to pick your battles. Few things are worth losing a friendship or business connection–or alienating a family member.

4.   Remember that many actions have contrary and some-times antagonistic reactions. In a contrary situation, always try to understand where the other person is coming from. That doesn't mean you have to agree, but at least try to understand the other person's point of view.

4. Schedule a Regular Date Night with Your Spouse.

Most of us love to have something to look forward to, and a scheduled date night is a great way to not only have an enjoyable evening with our better half, but also to explore different ways to spend time together. Many couples have a tendency to settle into the same old routine and don't change things up. A scheduled date night provides an opportunity to try new things, go new places, and meet new friends.

Here are some ways to make this happen:

1. Spouses should take turns planning each date night.

2. It's fun to tell your spouse about the plans, but it's also fun to keep them a surprise.

3. You know your spouse well (hopefully) so don't plan anything your significant other would even mildly object to. Be adventurous but stay within these boundaries.

4. Date Night should not normally include the kids, and most (if not all) conversations should be about you and your spouse, not the kids.

5. When your spouse plans the event, be open to new ideas and don't try to tell him or her what should have (or could have) been done to make it a better experience.

5. Develop Social Media Skills.

Social media, regardless of how we feel about it, plays a big role in our interactions with others. It can serve many purposes and it can be helpful in many ways, as long as it doesn't dominate our time and attention. You don't have to use all of the platforms; know enough about each one of them so you can decide which will benefit you in your interactions with others.

Consider these thoughts:

1. Social media platforms are a great way to stay in touch with others, especially those who live great distances from you.

2. Platforms such as LinkedIn are a great way to network career wise…just in case.

3. Don't share anything on social media you wouldn't want the whole world to know. You may be using privacy settings, but there is no such thing as privacy on the internet, and whatever is posted is essentially permanent. It can never be entirely retracted or deleted.

4. Learn to take a break from it so that it doesn't dominate your time.

6. Have a Close Friend You Trust Who is Well-Versed in Your Life.

We all need someone in our lives we can talk with, bounce ideas off, cry to, and cry with. Some call this person a confidant. This person needs to know us well but should not be a spouse, relative, or anyone who has skin in the game. It should undoubtedly be a person who has our best interests at heart, and someone who is not afraid to tell us when we are full of it, or that we are being stupid.

Interestingly, if you go out searching for this person, he or she probably won't be found. Instinctively, in the process of developing relationships, your confidant will become very evident, and quite possibly be someone you wouldn't really expect to take on the role.

7. Write Your Congressional Representative.

Amazingly, many laws have come about from letters written to a congressperson. It is of great benefit to not only know who government representatives are, but to also _interact with_ them. It can open new doors and expose us to those in a position to positively affect others.

Our congressional representatives are surprisingly approachable, and most have offices nearby that are also very welcoming. This provides a chance to become involved with a political process that can affect lives (hopefully) in a positive way. Public service and volunteerism can be incredibly rewarding. Engaging with others in a common purpose while learning through sharing ideas can provide enrichment at any age or stage in life.

8. Encourage Those Around You.

Anyone can criticize and point out mistakes. Don't be that person. Make it a point to encourage those with whom you interact often, but also be willing to encourage those you meet on a chance basis. You can have a very positive effect on someone else's life just by saying a kind word.

9. Learn the Fine Art of Arguing.

There is a right way to argue, and there are many WRONG ways. Here are some great tips about how to debate a subject without it getting out of hand:

1. Discuss disagreements but don't let anger fester for too long.
2. Talk about feelings before you get angry.
3. Don't raise your voice.
4. Don't do anything to threaten the relationship, particularly if you want to keep it.
5. Stay specific to the current concern. Don't bring up old issues.
6. Don't repress your anger, but don't let it take control.
7. Don't get baited into an argument; observe those who do this and avoid them.
8. Take a break if it gets crazy.
9. Pay attention to how your body is reacting, your heart rate, your body language, and the volume of your voice.
10. Develop a plan for resolution before an argument occurs.

There are many forms of arguing. Understanding how those close to you deal with conflict may make it easier to resolve any serious issues that come up.

With all that being said…

10. Don't Argue with A**holes.

One can usually tell who falls into this category. Be cordial but don't waste time and energy trying to convince these people–'nuff said.

11. Try This When You Don't Remember Someone's Name.

We've all been in this situation: You run into someone but cannot recall his or her name. There are two easy ways to handle this uncomfortable situation, provided your spouse or another person is with you. The first is to have your spouse introduce himself or herself to that person. The second, which is even easier, is to say, "Have you met my wife, Betty?" Unbelievably, the person will provide an introduction–works every time! (Well, almost!)

12. Consider These Techniques When Making Tough Phone Calls.

Many times, we find ourselves having to make phone calls that are difficult. One piece of advice is to resolve to do it and get it over with. Another helpful tip is to stand up and walk around while making the call. These two simple actions can help alleviate a lot of the pressure of delivering bad news, discussing frustrations, or even making tough decisions.

13. Be a "Careful Hugger."

In these days of overblown political correctness, abuse, and health concerns, it is wise to be very careful when (and especially how) you hug someone. Below are some thoughts on the subject:

1. If you don't know the person well, don't initiate. Don't assume it is OK. Better yet, let the other person make the first move.

2. In a "guy-girl" hug, make sure hands are not in inappropriate places, or even near a questionable area. Sometimes an arm around the upper shoulder, shoulder-to-shoulder side-hug is a better option.

3. Don't ever hug little kids unless you know them very well. It is best to ask the parents first, and then hug the child in front of his or her parents so they are assured that all is above board.

4. In a "guy-guy" hug, consider soul-shaking hands while embracing.

5. Don't let faces get too near.

6. Consider fist or elbow bumps, or "verbal hugs" instead of actual physical embraces.

(Author's note: Never underestimate the affection and meaning that can be conveyed in a firm, welcoming handshake. People should practice a good "business shake" as well as "friendly shakes" that convey true warmth and good will.)

14. Smile.

It's amazing what a little smile can do. Whether with people you know or people you meet for the first time, a smile can inject positivity into an encounter–even a dreadful one, like paying a bill or acknowledging an error. When smiling, make sure it's genuine and doesn't look phony. It helps to approach each person expecting the best, and a smile is a way to remind you to provide your best as well.

Even if you are wearing a mask, people can usually still tell if you are smiling. A real smile plays out in the eyes, too. Check it out in a mirror to see how it looks. You'll know you've reached someone if that person smiles back!

15. Listen to Others.

One of the greatest compliments you can pay someone is to *listen*. Too many times our minds are a hundred miles away during conversation. Too many times, also, we wait for someone to take a breath so we can immediately interject what we have been waiting impatiently to say.

People aren't always looking for a solution. Sometimes they just need to talk it out and *be heard*. Many times, people find their own answers just by having others listen to them. Speaking and hearing what is bottled within the heart and mind allow an individual to sort through a dilemma to determine solutions.

Being a willing listener pays great dividends for all parties involved. For the listener, it can expose the person to the critical-thinking skills necessary to address his or her own problems and provide insight when encountering similar situations.

16. Take Notes Visibly When in a Heated Discussion or Debate.

This action is so effective, and it really helps others to remain civil and more agreeable during an important discussion or disagreement. Make sure you conspicuously bring out your notepad and pen, so that the person knows you are taking notes on what's being said.

Amazingly, people will be more apt to soft-pedal the conversation and be more willing to find amicable solutions.

(Author's note: I've actually sat through meetings and scribbled meaninglessly while others were talking. The effect was the same!)

17. Pause in a Conversation Before Responding.

During any kind of conversation or discussion, regardless of its nature, always pause before responding. It lets the other conversant know you are listening closely and are seriously internalizing what they have said, not just trying to prove your point.

18. Learn to Deal with Toxic People.

In any situation with toxic people (and we've all had them), it's a good idea to learn a couple of tricks to move the situation along. This list contains a few:

1. Decide how important your involvement is. If it's not terribly necessary, get out before it gets obnoxious. If it is necessary, try to have an ally with you.

2. Take excellent notes so that the facts are not distorted and cannot come back to haunt you.

3. Keep the conversation as brief as possible. Sometimes, it is a good idea to start by indicating that you 'have a meeting in a few minutes, but wanted to just quickly confirm X or Y.' This will indicate that the conversation cannot extend, and it provides a previous excuse to end the meeting without appearing rude or dismissive, making the situation worse.

4. Try to find some common ground, no matter how difficult this might be. Be kind and cordial. You may even try asking the person's opinion on a topic.

5. Don't let others bait you into arguing or fighting.

6. Try to move an unproductive vein of discussion to closure.

7. When facing a volatile situation with someone ranting at you, stay quiet, let the individual finish, then continue to stay quiet. It has a way of reducing the

intensity of the moment and disarming the toxic individual.

8. Regardless of how loud the other person is, keep your own volume soft and calm, as this can trigger the person to be aware of his or her own overreaction.

19. Learn to Gracefully Bow Out of a Relationship.

There are many reasons and many situations where a person needs to exit a relationship, and it is important to make the experience as painless as possible for all parties. Depending on the situation, consider using these strategies in order to minimize the hurt caused:

1. Never end a relationship by text, social media, email, phone call, or even a handwritten note. It is a good idea to be in a public place, like a coffee shop or park, when having the discussion, as this helps maintain manners and decorum.

2. Don't go over the gory details of your reasons for ending the relationship. Keep these to a minimum.

3. Let the other person save face. Absorb blame if it helps the person accept the situation.

4. Try not to argue or defend your position. It usually never works.

5. Don't play the "blame game."

6. Be considerate of the other person's feelings.

7. Don't string the other person along. When it's time, do it.

8. Own up to your own mistakes.

9. Don't use lines like: "It was good while it lasted," "I wish it could have worked out," "It's not you, it's me," or "Can we still be friends?" If you say these things, the other person may double down on trying to repair or "fix" the deficiencies in the relationship. Be kind but be clear in your intentions.

20. Compliment Your Spouse At Least Three Times a Day.

Your spouse is probably the most important person in your life. Make it a point to be complimentary. It's actually very easy because you can always find something to compliment, as he or she is your partner in handling life and its many responsibilities. Really…could you do it all alone? Would you ever want to? It is important to acknowledge what that person brings to the table– the many talents and abilities that he or she adds to the loving partnership.

Here are some things to remember when complimenting your spouse:

1. Always be sincere with your compliments.

2. Try to look him or her in the eye when giving verbal compliments.

3. Consider using the B, B, B technique: Body, Brains, Beauty.

4. Try not to offer a compliment right after your spouse compliments you.

5. Brag about your spouse when he or she is not around. Amazingly, those words travel–and she or he will definitely hear about them. *(Author's Note: This does not count as one of the three compliments per day!)*

6. Consider the unique talents and personality traits your spouse has that complement (or quell) your own.

7. A small gift (e.g., chocolates, a rose, favorite snack, a card) that says "I was thinking of you today" could be the best compliment of all!

8. Work up to three compliments a day so you don't arouse any suspicions!

21. Refrain from Incessantly Talking About Yourself.

No one is more boring than someone who talks non-stop about himself of herself. We all know people who, every time you talk with them, they fill you in on every aspect of their lives. They want us to know *all things* about their kids, grandkids, what they are doing, who they are doing it with, all their aches and pains, and even each medical procedure they have had (or are considering). Sometimes they overshare with pictures as well.

Even if someone asks you how things are, be brief and move on to another relevant topic. Better yet, ask the person about his or her life. Most people will surely appreciate you focusing on them.

22. Don't Expect People to Change Their Minds–They Don't. They Make <u>New</u> Decisions Based on <u>New</u> Information.

Most people don't want to admit they are wrong. It's never fun to do so. Sometimes, even in the face of irrefutable evidence, a person will double down on a belief and simply adjust new information to suit the need to be correct, a phenomenon that experts call "confirmation bias." It is important to recognize this type of situation early in a discussion and save your breath.

Most people, however, when presented with new, compelling evidence to the contrary, do not have a problem adjusting a given point of view and at least becoming more openminded. It is certainly easier to say, "I didn't know that, and if I did, I never would've felt that way in the first place." It's a pride thing! We should foster this ability within ourselves, as well as be open to the possibility of our own adherence to confirmation bias.

It is important to be the type of person who assesses new evidence presented so we can adopt new approaches, just as it is beneficial to provide rational, fact-driven counterpoints when discussing controversial topics. Keep this in mind when involved in important decision-making discussions. Balance in each of these approaches allows a person to continue growing and learning with others. Admitting when you have reconsidered a position also surprises other people and can earn their respect.

23. Be Selective with Offensive Language.

Regardless of how acceptable offensive language is in your circle, use it sparingly, or not at all. There are many people who are offended by foul words and suggestive language, and so it is important that this does not become a habit, or it may come out or be overheard by someone to your detriment.

Here are some words of advice:

1. Make sure you know the group (or person) well before spewing offensive language.

2. Let others use it first before you start.

3. Be especially careful in mixed company.

4. Right or wrong, no matter what the group's composition, women who use foul language are usually looked down upon by others more quickly and more often.

5. If you do choose to use it, use it sparingly.

6. Try not use it to label or degrade a specific other person or group.

7. Never use offensive terms to speak about sex or a particular gender in a foul or disgusting manner.

8. Never use it in a business setting. It can be (and usually is) a major turnoff. It can also get you sent to Human Resources.

The best advice? Don't use offensive language for any reason or in any situation!

(Author's note: I've known of deals and transactions that were negated largely because one of the parties had a foul mouth.)

24. Maintain Balance if You Work at Home.

In these modern times, many people are very fortunate to work from their homes, rarely having to go to offices or job sites. Still others take a lot of work home with them after leaving a place of employment.

If you are one of the fortunate who can do some or all work from home, here are some suggestions to consider for balancing personal and professional life:

1. Set a time to start working and set a time to stop each day.

2. Get dressed just as you would if you were out in the work-a-day world (or close to it).

3. Have a dedicated work area that is away from distractions.

4. Stand up and take a break every so often.

5. Never attend a video conference dressed in a significantly more casual way than you would if you were having a conference room meeting–even if others do so.

6. Be aware of your background when video conferencing. Always sit at a desk and ensure the area that appears on camera is neat and professional looking.

7. Make a point to get out and spend quality time with others; do it as often as you can without sacrificing your effectiveness.

25. Keep Your Friends Close and Your Enemies Even Closer.

This aphorism is a great way to express the importance of knowing what your opposition is doing, regardless of the circumstances. In a business setting, it is vital that you stay on top of your competition. If there is a way to retain cordial communication with difficult individuals, it is beneficial to do so. In any adversarial situation, if you are really aware of the other person's stance, their values, and what strategies they use to be successful, you stand a much better chance of coming out on top if there is conflict.

In any type of relationship, it is important to know what other parties are doing and thinking so that you are better equipped to deal with situations and differences in opinion when these arise. Observing how people cope and react to day-to-day situations can provide a lot of information.

26. Engage with Children When They Come Home from School.

The time after school is essential for reconnecting with children–whether they are your own children or your grandchildren. They've had a long day and have been under the control of other people, different rules, and (often) less than supportive circumstances.

Follow these techniques to make the transition from school to home much easier and more meaningful:

1. Let the child blow off steam for a little while, on his or her own terms.

2. Let the child settle back in. Don't drill them with questions right away.

3. Ask open-ended questions instead of those that just require yes-or-no answers. For example: "What made your day really fantastic?" "Tell me the most interesting thing you learned today." "If you had it to

do all over again, what would you do to make this school day the best ever?"

4. Have a comfortable place at home to discuss the day's actual performance. You may want to consider having an office or study area set up with a desk or a little-used table to spread out books and lessons. Ask the child to show you what he or she learned and talk about it.

5. Discuss report cards individually before talking about these in front of siblings or friends.

6. Have a little incentive built into the child's performance (use your judgment on this and don't go overboard).

7. Spend a bit of time with each child individually to build his or her resiliency, confidence, and character.

8. Limit computer, TV, and phone time. Many families have scheduled media times for their kids (this varies with age).

9. Make time and ensure your child gets physical exercise.

10. Let children hear you say you love them–frequently each day–and not just when they are on their best behavior.

27. Give Your Spouse and Other Family Members Space.

As important as it is to spend time together, it is equally important that each family member has his or her own space to pursue interests. One grows exponentially and can even contribute better to the family unit if the person is able to spend time with others and is involved in outside activities. This space also gives children a chance to see other aspects of the world that they probably wouldn't be exposed to if they only spent time with the family.

28. Make Dinner Time Sacred.

Dinner is one of the few times a family, whatever it's make-up, has a chance to be together–_truly together._ Removing distractions is very important so the family can make this time, _quality time_.

One of the best strategies to use at this very important part of the day is to make sure that all phones are put away and inaccessible. So, unless a call is expected that will affect the whole family, it is better that no member of the family has a phone available…or even visible. This can be difficult when extended family is present, but it makes dinner so much more pleasurable and meaningful.

29. Make the Person You're with Feel Like He or She is the Only One in Your World.

When you are engaging with another person, give him or her your undivided attention. This can be difficult, but here are several tips to make interactions more natural:

1. Make and continue to hold eye contact with the person during conversation. Don't stare but provide meaningful affirmation that you are listening by facial expression and verbal cues.

2. Don't react to every other person who walks by or tries to get your attention.

3. Focus the conversation on the other person as much as possible.

4. Ignore your phone. If your phone rings, visibly silence the call. If you _have to answer_, excuse yourself and apologize for needing to accept the call. When the call is finished, apologize again for the interruption.

5. Make sure that when an encounter is finished, you reiterate to the person how great it was to see him or her and how much you are looking forward to spending time together again. If that is not the case, try to break off the meeting cordially.

30. Try This Strategy When Someone Wants to Talk and You Don't Have Time.

This idea was made popular by past President of the United States, Gerald Ford. Basically, if you are busy or in a hurry and someone approaches you wanting to talk, keep moving. If what the person has to say is important, he or she will continue to walk with you. If not, the individual will probably excuse themselves and catch you another time. This is a great way to handle an uncomfortable, tough situation without being rude.

31. Don't Feel Compelled to Explain Yourself to Others.

Everyone you encounter does not need to know what you are thinking or why you're doing what you are doing. Except for a few important people in your life, you don't owe an explanation for every decision you make. Those who like you and know you don't need an explanation; those who don't like you won't believe you anyway!

32. Ask Yourself: "What Difference Does It Make?"

People have a tendency to get into arguments over things that don't matter. Anytime you find yourself in a confrontation or disagreement, ask yourself if the outcome is all that important. If it is, be bold with your discussion points and work hard to convince the other party; however, if you recognize that it is not important or that you are just feeling a need to be right, make your points and move on. It's not always easy to do but staying in an argument just for argument's sake can be exhausting and, frankly, not worth the time and effort.

In Conclusion:

Learning to deal with people involves developing broad skills that play an incredibly important role in many facets of our lives. Similar encounters can be very comfortable or very unpleasant, depending on the reason for the meeting and the people involved–as well as your reaction to these variables. By utilizing these strategies, you can enhance your chances of accomplishing what you are trying to achieve within most relationships and have less conflict.

The most important person to develop a good relationship with is…YOU. When you know yourself and understand your principles and values, and are comfortable with your direction in life, you will look forward to spending time with others, sharing and learning as a community.

People are lonely because they build walls
instead of bridges.

—Joseph F. Newton
Author and Minister

FINANCIAL STRATEGIES

"Money is only a tool. It will take you wherever you wish,
but it will not replace you as the driver."

–Ayn Rand
Author and Philosopher

"For the love of money is the root of all evil," is one of the most often misquoted and misunderstood verses in the Bible. These misinterpretations have caused many people to live lives of unnecessary discomfort and turmoil.

Simply put, money is a tool–nothing more, nothing less. It can be used to secure our lives and help others to live better. If we approach money in this fashion, we can plan to have lives of comfort, or at least to have more security and certainty. When individuals use money appropriately, it can provide safety and stability, but also greater freedom. We are less of a burden on others and more independent when we take responsibility for our own finances–but further, when we have this independence, we are better able to assist others.

Of course, money can also be used to cause great harm. There are many pitfalls on the road to financial success. If the pursuit of money is the only focus, we may, at some point, struggle with the reality that our priorities have become warped.

With all that being said, it is ultimately *your responsibility* to secure your financial future and pave the way to personal financial freedom. If we can't help ourselves, we won't be in a position to help others.

There are many sound financial strategies, both long and short term, that can help put a person in a better position to deal with tough situations that can unexpectedly upend life.

In this chapter, you will find many great tips and strategies to help you acquire and save money, enabling you to feel the comfort and security of financial freedom. Many strategies are able to be applied right away, while others may not become factors until later in life. Still others may just give you peace of mind, knowing that you are prepared to handle any fiscal challenges life throws your way.

Be bold but not reckless!

1. Build and Maintain an Emergency Fund.

Stuff happens. We lose jobs; we need expensive auto repairs; a child has a tooth knocked out in a soccer game... Surprises are part of life. As much as we would like to, we can't always control what happens. The good news is that we can be prepared for the possibilities. If we have the wherewithal to pay for these surprises without having to borrow or make sacrifices, we are far ahead in the game.

Financial experts such as Dave Ramsey suggest that we have at least four to six months of living expenses put away in an ***emergency fund***. This is a safe account that is readily accessible and available for any occasion (e.g., an interest-bearing savings account or a CD). Financial experts don't suggest you "put cash under the mattress," so to speak, but it is key to have this money readily available and not tied into investments or assets that would need to be liquidated. This ***emergency fund*** should be the first account you fully fund; even before a retirement account, or before starting to pay off debts in general. This fund is a hedge against financial ruin, and thus, it is the most important first step to take in creating financial stability.

An emergency fund won't take away the pain of tough situations, but it can help provide a buffer to make intelligent decisions and keep a family afloat during a rough spell.

2. Keep a "Slush Fund."

The purpose of a ***slush fund*** is totally different than the ***emergency fund***. While the emergency fund is designed to help in difficult situations, the slush fund is put away to have enough money available to fund something (e.g., an opportunity, trip, or big item) that would probably be considered frivolous–something that is not essential, but that you would really like. It has little to do with anything you ***need*** but is something you ***want***. This account allows for splurging. If you have already set aside the money and it doesn't affect your overall financial picture, an occasional splurge is OK.

It is a good idea to "sleep on" a slush fund purchase for a couple days before committing to it. If you do decide to make the move, enjoy your choice, knowing you could truly afford it!

> *(Author's Note: There are many ways to start and maintain a slush fund. There are apps available that will move the "change remainder" of a whole dollar from each purchase made. Even the good old-fashioned "change jar" could be utilized for this purpose!)*

3. Develop a Budget and Stick to It.

A budget is a great tool to use for many reasons. Basically, it starts with creating a list that shows where and how every penny you earn is used. After you are aware of how you are using your money, you can identify goals based on what your **needs** are. Additionally, you can evaluate the expenditures you are making that address **wants** and determine if any of these might be reduced. This process can be illuminating and helps with developing discipline in spending habits.

Oftentimes, just foregoing certain purchases (or waiting for better timing) and reducing (or eliminating) debt can help a person achieve financial prosperity. Budgeting is the first step to finding the "change in the cushions" to help make this possible.

Here are some great ideas to use when developing a budget and sticking with it:

1. Make sure all financial decision-makers close to you are on board with the budgetary principles introduced and that these individuals help in the development of the budget.

2. Don't just make a budget and keep it in your head. It is vital to have all expenditures and goals written out.

3. Allocate how much is needed for each financial necessity, such as housing, food, utilities, transportation and debt reduction (e.g., paying off credit cards or a mortgage early). Each family will have its own unique needs.

4. Try to have a little "play money" built into the budget. Trying to be overly strict can reduce buy-in.

5. Let children be a part of developing the budget. It's never too early to start educating them about money.

6. Review and make any necessary adjustments to the budget on a quarterly basis (or more frequently if necessary).

7. Celebrate when you pay off a major debt.

   (Author's Note: Debt reduction, with a goal of being totally debt free, should be a major goal of any budget.)

4. Restrict Withdrawals from Retirement Accounts When Retired.

It is essential to leave retirement accounts alone so they can continue to grow. Life expectancy today is longer than it was for earlier generations, so it is important to have as much available in these accounts as possible as we become more dependent on others for life's necessities.

It is still an effective guideline to withdraw no more than four to four-and-a-half percent from retirement accounts per year so as not to deplete them too quickly. The markets routinely average at least this same percentage in growth per year over the long haul, so the idea is to protect the principal amount and not spend it down.

Of course, there may be extenuating circumstances. At some point you may need to start taking out more from these accounts. But until that time, be stingy with these savings and protect them as much as you can.

5. Review and Compare Auto Insurance Rates at Least Every Other Year.

Auto insurance companies have a tendency to raise rates yearly. They also add or remove parts of policies, and these changes could affect you. It is a good idea to compare the rates and benefits of different companies to take advantage of savings.

It is important to make sure you compare "apples to apples" when looking at policies and get a *quote in writing* from the agent. It's amazing the discounts that just "appear" when an agent knows you are shopping!

(Author's note: This is also true with cable and internet providers, as well as cell phone service companies.)

6. Carry an Umbrella Policy.

If you have over $100,000 in assets, it is wise to consider holding an umbrella insurance policy. For approximately $300-500 per year, an umbrella policy provides peace of mind, knowing that your assets are protected from unforeseen events, such as a tragic accident, in which you could be held responsible for damages or bodily injury.

Your automobile or home insurance agent is a good source of information concerning these types of policies, and if you piggyback them with your auto or home coverage, they are usually more reasonable in cost.

7. Start A Small Business on the Side.

No matter how busy a person is, there is usually time to be involved in other activities. Why not use the extra time to start a small business? Even if it only generates a small amount of profit, it may turn into something more lucrative. It could even become something you turn over to your children as an introduction to the real world of business. This actually happens over and over again: someone starts a small, part-time, hobby-type business that grows into a profitable enterprise, and then decisions have to be made whether to continue it as a hobby or turn it into a primary stream of income.

8. Don't Borrow from Your Retirement.

Unless it is a matter of life-or-death, never borrow or withdraw from your retirement, even if you are already retired. You've worked hard to accumulate a nice nest egg for later years, but it is difficult to make that up if you use it too early.

There are many reasons people borrow money from a 401K or 403b, but few of them are good enough to justify the move. Many borrow from their accounts to buy a car, make a down payment on a house, fund their kids' college education, or take a fantastic vacation. It is better to borrow from a lending institution than to take from your retirement. Not only do you have to pay taxes on the amount withdrawn, but you also miss out on the interest being paid over the years of your life. Don't take money from the principle of your retirement unless you have literally no other option.

> *(Author's Note: Do not do a reverse mortgage. As great as they sound on TV, they are basically a trap!)*

9. Pay Bills Online and On Time.

As much as you can, pay your bills online. It is so much easier and it allows you to monitor account activity. If you choose, you can have hardcopy receipts sent to you, but you will always have an e-trail of what's been paid at your fingertips. It is important to make sure you have a live person you can chat with while paying online. Be sure to preview your payments before hitting the pay button. Some places even give you a discount for paying online.

Also: Pay on time. Never allow yourself to be hit with late fees and added interest.

10. Consider the Possibility that You May Require Long-Term Care.

If a person is blessed with longevity, he or she is likely to face the question of how to deal with long-term care (LTC). This concern should be addressed well in advance to ensure the best decisions are made.

According to the US Department of Health and Human Services (2020) and Elder Law Answers (2016):

1. People generally do not require long-term care until the age of 80-85.

2. If a person does need it, there's a 42 to 44 percent chance it will be needed for less than one year.

3. There is a 25 percent chance that an individual's stay in a long-term care facility will last more than three

years. There is a 20 percent chance that it will last more than five years.

4. Eating a healthy diet, remaining physically active, and managing health concerns are the best defenses against requiring long-term care.

Keep in mind that these are only odds. Anything can happen, so it's important to be prepared for all eventualities. There are two basic ways to pay for long-term care. A person can purchase LTC insurance or it can be self-funded. There are pros and cons to each path, so it's important to do the research and mold your selected program around your lifestyle and capabilities. Here are some thoughts and considerations regarding LTC:

1. If you don't need long-term care, you will probably have a much bigger nest egg late in life.

2. If you are healthy and work to stay that way, the odds are strongly in your favor that you will not need long-term care.

3. LTC insurance policies often do not guarantee that their costs will remain constant throughout the term of the policy.

4. If you start saving early to self-insure for LTC, you should be able to put away a substantial amount. If you invest the value of what the premiums would be for LTC insurance, the chances are good that you would have enough to self-fund long-term care. It's a smart

idea to keep this money in a separate account and contribute to it consistently.

5. Whatever your decision, it is important to discuss these options with a certified elder care attorney or expert who does _not_ sell LTC insurance to help you decide the best path.

It is important to consider the possibility of needing long-term care and making provisions for financial independency, as you do not want to be a burden on your children. If you start preparing early for your late-in-life care and are consistent with this process, you will live your years feeling more secure about your future.

11. Receive a Free Credit Report Each Year.

A person is entitled to a free credit report once a year from each of the three credit-reporting agencies: Equifax, Experian, and TransUnion. The credit score, also called a Fair Isaac Corp. (FICO) score, is a three-digit number based on a formula that is designed to gauge credit worthiness. A low credit score can result in many financial problems. It can:

1. Cost a person thousands more when taking out a mortgage, car, or student loan, or even keep a person from qualifying for a loan.

2. Keep a person from qualifying for a lease.

3. Prevent an individual from landing the great job he or she has always wanted and is otherwise qualified for.

4. Be a sign of fraudulent activity on an individual's accounts.

It is very easy to obtain a free credit report, and it should be done annually, if for no other reason but to ensure that all is well.

12. Use, Don't Abuse, Credit Cards.

Credit cards can be a curse when used inappropriately; they can be a blessing if used sensibly. Their convenience is undeniable. They provide a great way to monitor spending; however, misuse can put a person into deep financial trouble and can affect a person's long-term financial outcomes. According to *USA Today*, the average American holds over $6,200 in credit card debt (Picchi, 2020). This kind of burden can alter a person's ability to make prudent financial decisions, particularly if it is compounded by other forms of debt, such as a college loan, car loan, and mortgage.

Part of the reason credit card debt continues to explode is that credit card companies have continually raised credit limits, such that the average credit limit is now over $31,000 (Picchi, 2020). High credit limits combined with undisciplined spending habits can entrap individuals in a mountain of debt and cause financial ruin.

To avoid these misfortunes, use credit cards as an important financial tool by following these strategies:

1. Use cards with rewards programs attached. You can usually find one or two that fit into your lifestyle.

2. Use cards as a way to monitor spending habits and more easily follow your budget.

3. Understand the billing cycle to make it easier to make payments on time.

4. Start paying off credit cards as soon as you can at the end of each month. In other words: don't carry a balance.

5. Use cards that have purchase insurance attached to them.

6. Make sure your card does not start charging interest at the point of purchase. (This is rare, but it still occurs.)

7. Check outside card readers (e.g., gas stations) to make sure there are no illicit scanning devices present.

8. Use mainly one card but have two different cards in case a vendor does not accept your preferred card.

9. Avoid store-specific cards, even if they offer a "teaser rate" or a special discount on a purchase. Store-specific cards often have high interest rates and unused cards can possibly lower a credit score.

10. Monitor accounts at least every other day in order to detect any possible fraudulent activity.

11. Except in an **extreme** emergency, do not take a cash advance from a card company.

12. Make payments on time. Avoid late payments at all costs.

With that being said…

Using a debit card is a great alternative, and some debit cards have many of the same benefits as a credit card. Additionally, using a debit card ensures that the person does not spend outside his or her means. When using a debit card:

1. Never let it out of sight.

2. Always use the credit option and don't put in the pin number.

3. Use it for smaller-priced purchases, as debit card purchases do not usually have insurance attached.

13. Put Any Windfall toward Debt Reduction.

Anytime you come into some extra money and you have debt, this should be used to pay down debt balances. But be sure to save a little of the extra earnings for a nice evening out, rewarding frugality, hard work, and another step toward your debt-reduction goals.

14. Never Co-Sign a Personal Loan for Another Person.

Except in rare cases, it is very dangerous to co-sign a personal loan with another party. Basically, it puts the other person in control of a portion of your finances and, if that person defaults or gets behind in the loan payments, it could put your credit in jeopardy.

If someone you know and love truly needs the money and has no other source but you, it is best to borrow the money in your name and have the person pay you back directly. In this case, it is critical to draw up a contract with the individual first. If it is for a sum you can spare, it might be better to consider gifting it to the person rather than cosigning a loan. As mentioned before, a person should _never_ borrow money from retirement accounts, whether retired or not.

15. Start and Maintain Your "Trusted Vendor" List.

This list is invaluable. If something goes wrong, it is critical to have a name or organization at your fingertips who can be contacted and trusted to provide assistance or guidance.

There are companies that specialize in finding vendors, but keep in mind that the people being referred pay these "finding companies" to be on their lists. Many times, these vendors are not local or are not adequately acceptable in their services to garner their own business consistently.

Your vendor list will change over the years, but developing a good relationship with people you trust will guarantee better workmanship simply because they know you are a repeat customer. Chances are they will even give you a break in pricing.

16. Manage a Mortgage, but Don't "Marry Your Home."

A mortgage is a great tool if utilized correctly. It can help you get into a home and build equity, or it can cause you to become "married to your house." Many people borrow too much to purchase a home and end up having an inordinate amount of income go to paying for and maintaining this dream home. This can make a person resent the decision to buy the home in the first place.

If you are thinking about borrowing to pay for a home, consider these strategies:

1. Do not select a home that will require you to devote more than 30 percent of your income to housing. That percentage should include the mortgage, property taxes, utilities, upkeep of the house, and HOA fees.

2. Spend as much time shopping for a mortgage as you spend looking for a house.

3. Do not consider an adjustable-rate mortgage unless you are certain you will not be living in the house for more than five years.

4. Save up and put 20 percent down on the cost of the home (or more) at the time of purchase.

5. Put yourself in a position to purchase a 15-year mortgage. If you must have a 30-year mortgage, double up on your payments or make an extra payment

or two each year. Make sure you direct any extra payments towards the principal.

6. Don't just shop interest rates. They can be lower but have overall higher expenses. Compare "apples to apples" when selecting an option.

7. Deal with a reputable lender and make sure you have a local contact available if you use a national mortgage company.

8. Consider having a trusted real estate attorney peruse all the documents before signing.

9. Research the different types of loan programs available. There are many available today with little or no upfront charges.

10. Always keep in mind that rates and terms are negotiable.

17. Use GoodRX for Prescriptions.

If you are interested in saving money on prescriptions, GoodRX is a great program that is very easy to use. If you run a search through GoodRX for the prescription you are purchasing, it will tell you what you would pay for it at various pharmacies. It's that simple!

18. Do Not Allow Your Vehicle to Be a Money Pit.

Vehicles can be a major money pit. As you drive them off the new showroom floor, they depreciate in value by approximately 30 percent–and that's just the beginning. Depending on the type and model, and how long you keep the car, an automobile can cost you untold amounts of money and lost time.

Although a vehicle is a necessity for most, there are some things that can be done to lessen the financial burden of automobile ownership:

1. Consider buying a previously owned vehicle. This lessens the depreciation of a new purchase, and with some effort, you can find an option that is nearly new.

2. Research brands and models to find out which ones are more economical to operate and maintain.

3. There are almost no good reasons to lease a car, but there are _a lot_ of bad ones.

4. Buy a car you can afford, with cash, if possible.

5. Learn to perform many of the basic maintenance procedures yourself. Over the course of the life of the car, this will save a lot of money.

6. Get a diagnostic reader and use it when the engine light comes on or when you suspect a mechanical problem. There are units available for less than $100 that link to your phone. They even tell you approximately what a repair should cost.

7. Shop around for automobile insurance and use a plan with a higher deductible.

8. Consider car models that run on lower-octane fuel.

9. Be sure to calculate the break-even point regarding the purchase price and fuel savings if considering an electric car. Also, explore the range restrictions and locations of charging stations.

10. Consider not even owning a vehicle if you live in a major municipality. Rides are readily available through ride-sharing services such as Uber and Lyft.

11. Use mass transit whenever possible to save on gas, wear and tear on the car, and parking fees.

12. Consider sharing car ownership with a family member, friend, or neighbor.

19. Read the Fine Print.

There are countless examples of situations where people did not heed this advice and ended up getting burned. Consider having a trusted attorney read over any major document before you sign on the dotted line–'nuff said!

20. Research and Compare Medicare Supplement and Advantage Plans.

One of the biggest expenses incurred in the mature years is healthcare. Medicare is a great blessing for those who paid into the program, but it is not usually enough to cover all or even most medical expenses as a person grows older. This is the reason for the Supplement and Advantage plans.

There are pros and cons to both Supplement and Advantage plans. When doing research, make sure to select one that fits your lifestyle and covers what you need covered. Some plans have no upfront costs but have a copay, and only cover a certain percentage of expenses. Others have a premium but cover all expenses. Some can still be used while you travel, while others are tied to one or two local medical facilities.

When researching plans, make sure to consult with experts who deal with many types of plans and are not tied to just one company or program. There are many senior organizations available to help with these decisions. It is important to provide the time to research in advance, rather than waiting until the last minute and trying to make informed choices. Additionally, these plans may change coverage benefits every year, so it is imperative that you revisit them on an annual basis.

21. Live Below Your Means: Don't Try to "Keep Up with the Joneses."

Just because your neighbor or brother lives a lavish lifestyle, it doesn't mean you have to try to live up to these standards. This is one of the most dangerous mistakes a person can make and could lead to financial ruin. It is not just an old adage–people really should always try to live below their means, regardless of what their finances are. According to a recent study by *CareerBuilder*, nearly 78 percent of individuals in the workforce live paycheck to paycheck (Martin, 2019). It is easy to yearn for the extras that others have, but if you were allowed to draw back the curtain, you would likely find that many of your "rich" neighbors or friends are actually living month to month and don't know how to escape a cycle of constant overspending and debt–including all the inevitable financial stress. Unfortunately, while they really do know the solution, pride won't let them solve it. They just don't want to admit that they're broke and need to stop spending! The real secret to happiness is looking around at the life you have built–family, friends, and the all you have worked for–and realizing that you truly already have all that you need.

22. Have an Energy Audit for Your Home and Business.

Most municipalities will do a complimentary energy audit on a home, and possibly on a place of business as well. This is a great way to see if you have any appliances or equipment that are no longer efficient or have leaks that could be causing added operating expenses.

Ask questions of the inspector as he or she checks your systems. You will probably learn a lot of cost-saving tips and strategies that apply directly to the properties you own.

23. Rarely Buy an Extended Warranty.

Extended warranties are great money makers–*for the people selling them.* Regardless of what you are purchasing and regardless of what the salesman tells you, an extended warranty is rarely, if ever, worth its cost–or the paper it is printed on, for that matter. Many products have a built-in warranty plan, and many credit cards have a warranty period that kicks in at the point of purchase.

Save yourself some money and avoid the extra expense of an extended warranty.

24. Consider Contributing to A Health Savings Account (HSA).

A Health Savings Account (HSA) allows an individual to set aside funds on a pre-tax basis to pay for qualified medical expenses. Although these accounts normally cannot be used to pay for insurance premiums, they can be used to cover deductibles, copayments, prescriptions, over-the-counter medications, and other medical expenses. In order to qualify for this type of account, the person must have a High Deductible Health Plan (HDHP) that only covers preventive services before the deductible.

Health Savings Accounts are not for everyone. It is important to research options and confer with a trusted financial advisor to see if one is the right fit for you.

(Author's note: For more information on HSAs, search for Publication 969 at IRS.gov.)

25. Don't Own the Biggest House on the Block.

When buying a home, don't purchase the biggest and most expensive one in the neighborhood. This not only puts you at odds with your neighbor but also makes the house (and your vehicles) a target for break ins. Generally speaking, it makes it more difficult to sell the house in the future and you probably won't get the home's full value when you do put it on the market.

26. Take Social Security Only When You Really Need It.

When to begin taking from Social Security is a big decision. A person can begin taking it as early as 62 years old (as of 2020), but there are other variables to consider and many options available. The following are some aspects to compare when making a decision:

1. The earlier it is taken, the smaller the monthly amount will be, but the person will likely draw from it for an overall longer period of time.

2. The later it is taken, the larger the monthly amount will be, but the person will probably draw from it for a shorter period of time overall.

3. When a person's spouse dies, the other individual receives the higher of the two accounts (if they are a legal couple).

4. If a person is still earning income, the Social Security benefit is reduced until he or she is 66 years old (as of 2020). At that age, the individual can have any amount of income and the Social Security benefit is not penalized.

5. Probably the best decision is to start taking Social Security when a person actually needs it. If an individual doesn't need it immediately, it might be good to start at the age of 70. This is where it is capped (as of 2020).

The Social Security System is constantly being addressed by Congress and changes are often being proposed, so it is important to stay current on any modifications that may occur.

27. Take Advantage of Scholarships and Educational Programs Available.

There are so many scholarships available today, and contrary to popular belief, they are available to almost anyone. Most states and the federal government make these opportunities available to those who need them and those who earn them. There are also many foreign-student scholarships accessible to international students who would like to study in the United States. These scholarships are reciprocally available to United States citizens wishing to study abroad.

Amazingly, there are also opportunities for adults of any age who would like to further their studies. Serving four years in the military usually qualifies an individual for the *GI Bill,* which provides tuition with a stipend to former service members and their families. Senior citizens are able to audit classes at local universities, usually at little or no expense.

Additionally, if an individual is involved in certain professions where there is a market to teach that topic, many institutions provide an option to attend classes while serving as a faculty member. Some companies even offer tuition reimbursement programs.

With that being said…

28. Be Wary Regarding Student Loans.

Student-loan debt is currently the largest debt in the United States today. These loans are readily available to almost anyone who is willing to go through the hassle of applying. Unfortunately, many young adults today graduate from college with massive loans to pay off. This is not a great way to start a career.

Here are some considerations to address before getting involved in a student loan:

1. There are many other ways to finance a college education (reread above).

2. It is often a good strategy to attend school part time while working in a company or field you ultimately hope to advance within. This allows you to network and gain experience while progressing to a degree.

3. Many occupations do not compensate a person enough to comfortably pay off a large student loan without causing financial hardship, so the program of study is an important facet in considering a loan.

4. Student loan debt is NOT forgiven in bankruptcy proceedings.

5. It is a good idea to explore programs that allow a student to attend college while training or interning in a specific field. Many companies will help pay for an employee's education if he or she shows promise and commits to a few years working for them after graduating.

6. If a person must finance a college course of study, consider using unsecured loans, if these are available, for this purpose.

7. You can also work before starting higher education and put away a nice "education nest egg." This could take a lot of pressure off and even help you decide what profession you would ultimately love to be a part of.

8. Consider taking the first two years of classes at a community college and transferring. Generally, the tuition and commuting expenses are half that of a university and a much smaller fraction of a private college. It also eliminates the housing cost if the person must board at the university in order to attend.

9. Consider a trade school. These are usually much more reasonable in terms of cost and provide individuals with excellent trades that pay well, often through short-term training taking only a few months. Additionally, many trade schools and local colleges offer college credit for certifications offered, allowing an individual to apply these toward a college degree if desired. This could provide an opportunity to work and go to school for later career advancement.

29. Prepare for the Required Minimum Distribution (RMD).

When a person reaches the age of 72.5 (as of the year 2020) he or she is required to withdraw a certain amount from his or her retirement accounts and pay taxes on this money. The amount is based on each account's balance at the end of the previous year; this must be withdrawn during the next calendar year.

There are many ways to handle the RMD. Many people take the money out, pay the taxes and then reinvest the balance.

Others take a sweet vacation using these funds. Whatever the strategy selected, it is important to be aware that a person can and will be penalized if he or she does not follow through yearly on this federal requirement.

30. Prepare Your Significant Other if You Are in a Committed Relationship.

Many couples have no idea what would happen if one of them was suddenly removed from the picture. We've all seen it: A spouse passes away and the other has no idea how to do many of the tasks that this person normally performed. This compounds an already heartbreaking situation for the person.

Below is a partial list of important information that must be shared and made available to your spouse (or significant other) in order to lessen the pain and aggravation of separation:

1. A list of all bank accounts including locations, passwords, and security answers, as well as the trusted advisor used for each.

2. A list of all recurring bills that are paid, how they are paid, and approximately how much is involved.

3. The location of all insurance policies, birth certificates, mortgages, vehicle titles, and any other pertinent documents.

4. A list of trusted vendors used over the years.

5. A *Living Will*, durable *Power of Attorney,* and *Do Not Resuscitate Order* (DNR). Having a trust is always a consideration.

6. Any funeral and burial requests and arrangements previously made.

7. Access to computer and cell phone passwords.

8. A *Last Will and Testament.* (For this, make sure you have an original copy.)

9. An understanding of the state's or country's probate laws and how they apply to your specific situation.

10. The location of any extraordinary documents or funds that the person may not be aware of (e.g., stocks, bonds, and 401K or other accounts).

11. If you are not in a committed relationship, it is important to make sure you have someone close to you who has access to all of your information and is aware of your wishes

The best advice is to avoid being one of those couples who believe they have plenty of time to gather and coordinate this information with each other, and then the worst happens, leaving them unable to handle all of these aspects while grieving. Life can take some crazy twists and turns. It is important to spend some time together going over and preparing these documents and making sure you both know how to handle the finances. There is a peace in having the future handled, and you will feel so much more secure in your relationship knowing that what you *can control* of such a loss has been managed with clear, calm, and careful steps–together.

31. Do Your Own Lawn Care.

If you are physically able, it is a great idea to spend the time yourself to keep up your lawn and landscaping. There are many health and emotional benefits to being outdoors; plus, you will save a LOT of money! It's good exercise and will even give an opportunity to express creativity. It can also become a social event, because it gives you a chance to talk to the neighbors and even spend time with your spouse or family members if they come out to join you.

32. Use Coupons and Become a Savvy Shopper.

Most stores (both online and brick and mortar) have an ample supply of coupons available to customers. These can provide savings when you compare purchases over a long period of time. Hundreds and possibly thousands of dollars can be saved each year if a person is willing to collect and organize coupons for access and use. Some grocery stores even allow a person to "stack" together manufacturer's coupons with their own store-issued coupons (or those of a competitor), and many printable coupons are available online through couponing websites that can teach you even more tricks of the trade.

(Author's note: Caution–Couponing can be habit-forming!)

33. Diversify Investments.

It's never a good idea to have all your financial eggs in one basket. When you consider the constant fluctuations in the markets, it is important to spread assets into different categories in order to limit the effect of market downturns–but also to benefit from upticks. Some strategies to keep investments productive include:

1. A person should invest on a consistent basis (i.e., dollar-cost average).

2. The younger a person is, the larger should be the percentage of assets in more aggressive investments. Early in a career, a person can take on a larger risk-to-reward investment gamble (within reason, of course).

3. As a person grows older, he or she should consider moving assets into less aggressive investment tools. (Don't do this too soon.)

4. It is important to take advantage of an employer's matching-funds investment options. If a person must leave that place of employment, the investments should move with the person.

5. Real estate can be a great investment, but it does have its pitfalls. Before investing in real estate, one should

always consider the "hassle factor," and how this will affect other life duties, travel, and other assets.

6. If possible, a person should invest in a Roth Individual Retirement Account (Roth IRA). This is an investment account that is not taxed upon distribution, as long as certain conditions are met.

7. It is important to compare 12b-1 fees (and others) when choosing investment tools. The 12b-1 fees are those paid out from the account or asset to cover the cost of distribution, marketing, or selling shares, or providing shareholder services.

8. Consider buying stocks that pay dividends. A stock dividend is a benefit paid to shareholders that can be used to purchase additional stock or can be taken in cash.

   (Author's note: Many retirees live off of or supplement their income using stock dividends.)

9. It's usually not a good idea to view insurance policies as investment tools.

10. Don't fall for the latest investment scheme of the month.

11. Find a competent financial advisor who is on top of the newest trends. Don't be afraid to ask him or her to explain recommendations and be honest about your investment goals.

(Author's Note: The best investment advice ever? Buy when the masses say "sell." And sell when the masses say "buy!")

34. Monitor Retirement Accounts Sparingly.

Do yourself a favor and don't check your retirement accounts too frequently. This can be a frustrating experience and cause you to second guess some of your well-planned decisions. Some ideas to consider:

1. When you first start investing, monitor the accounts closely to make sure your investment facilitator aligned the selections as you instructed.

2. Don't revisit investments every time there's a turn in the market. Markets are generally a long-term investment tool, so watching every dip and change generally just causes unnecessary stress over normal, expected fluctuations.

3. Monitor accounts every few weeks to make sure there is no outside interference. This is usually not a problem if you invest with a legitimate investment organization.

4. If an advisor is "churning" your accounts without your permission, you probably should consider changing advisors.

(Author's Note: Churning refers to the practice of a broker conducting excessive trading in a client's account mainly to generate commissions.)

Meet with your trusted financial advisor (or at least talk with him or her) on a quarterly basis. Sit down with your advisor face to face at least once a year if possible.

35. Be Knowledgeable and Practical about Life Insurance.

Buying life insurance can be a daunting task. There are so many factors, approaches, and products to consider. It is a good bet that most people will need life insurance at some point, but it takes some extensive research and soul searching to make the best decision about the type and amount of insurance held. It is important to consider these aspects when attempting to make an educated decision about this major purchase:

1. Understand *why* you are considering the purchase of life insurance. What do you need it to cover? Consider how long and for what period of time this funding will be needed.

2. Understand the differences between *term-life* and *whole-life* policies. Most life insurance policies fall into one of these categories.

3. Consider how much coverage you actually need. Most insurance companies have assessment calculators to help make this determination.

4. Be reasonable with your expectations. Your life insurance rate is based on you, your needs, and your health. It is important to be completely honest about all of these.

5. Don't put off this purchase. The longer you wait, the more expensive it becomes to obtain insurance, and you certainly do not want your loved ones left unprotected.

6. Life changes, and the coverage you have needs to reflect these changes. It is a good idea to review your coverage every one or two years.

7. Review the policy very closely and ask questions before you sign.

8. Carefully consider policies with living benefits. Even though they add charges to a premium, they may well fit the lifestyle needs of you and your family.

9. Be aware that many employers provide life insurance at little or no cost to their employees.

10. Use a trusted financial advisor to help you choose the right agent for you.

Generally speaking, it is a good approach to buy term-life insurance and invest the difference between the cost of that policy and an equivalent whole-life policy. There are obviously other approaches, but this is a very popular way for people to protect their loved ones and not overspend.

In Conclusion:

Whether we like it or not, money is a major driving force in our lives. Many (if not most) decisions are affected by it. Here are some general guidelines concerning money and its place in our lives:

1. It's better to have more money than less!

2. Save and strive to reach a point in life where money does not control most of your decisions.

3. Always pay yourself first.

4. If you are considering a major purchase, research and address all the factors, and then sleep on the decision for at least 48 hours.

5. Regardless of the person or his or her expertise, don't let others control your money.

6. Teach your kids about money and investing.

7. Live below your means.

8. Internalize the difference between a _need_ and _want_, and then classify purchases into these categories in order to prioritize.

9. Be prepared for rainy days–they will come.

10. Support a charity and become involved with it in some capacity. One of the great benefits of being financially stable is being able to support causes you believe in; sharing generously with those who are in need.

11. Be the most generous person you know.

I've been rich, and I've been poor...rich is so much better
– Many take credit for this quote!

CHAPTER SEVEN

PSYCHOLOGICAL STRATEGIES

*"Life is 5% what happens to us and
95% how we deal with it."*

–Anonymous

The term "psychology" means many things to many people. For the sake of simplicity and organization, this book approaches psychology as the involvement of the human mind in its reaction to events, and how this can affect behavior.

We all have burdens, and many of these are magnified or exaggerated based on our perception of their effects on our life, our potential, and our ability to be successful in given situations. Many of these burdens may hold us back from accomplishing what we otherwise could. It is important to recognize the effect of some of these burdens and take action to remove them, or at least put them "on the back burner."

For some traumatic situations, it is a long and difficult process to negate or eliminate these effects, and it may be necessary to involve professional help and commit to a period of serious counselling and soul searching. For other, less serious, and less impactful situations, it is possible for short-term measures, such as changes in behavior or outlook, to alleviate their effects. Regardless of the situation, it is important to recognize and identify what needs to be done and follow through with these corrective measures.

This chapter provides many strategies that are effective in dealing with life's smaller challenges, be they self-induced or externally produced. There are also strategies to combat more seriously debilitating problems. ***Keep in mind, there is no substitute for working with an experienced professional who is trained in helping individuals confront and resolve their concerns.*** Professionals are readily available for consult. While some people may read this advice and throw out excuses for not wanting to work with someone to alleviate issues, having someone advise you on how to resolve concerns is no different than having a financial expert lead you through investment decisions or having a doctor help determine treatment for a physical ailment. Going to an experienced social worker, psychologist, or therapist is <u>an investment in YOU</u>– in your happiness and growth as a person. To make the most of your life, it is essential to use <u>all the tools</u> at your disposal to feel great about who you are and the life you are living.

That being said, many tools for self-improvement start with just setting your mind toward the right "channel" or attitude and sticking with it. We are truly our own worst critics, so if just one of these strategies lessens a burden you have been living with, it would well be worth the cost, time, or energy expended. This way you can live freer and with more acceptance of who you are.

1. Remember the Past, but Don't Dwell on It.

The past is part of our lives and makes up much of who we are now. Taking just a single piece away could affect all of what we have achieved–including our relationships–in both good *and bad* ways. While there may be parts of the past we are not proud of, there is nothing we can do to change it. It is important to recognize this so that the past does not control our lives today–or going forward.

One good way to recognize if a past situation is seriously affecting a person is if it is keeping the individual from getting a good night's sleep or repeating in the person's thoughts over an extended period of time. If this is the case, it is best to see a counsellor to help deal with the situation. Pain, guilt, or trauma that plagues the mind and heart drains happiness and productivity from a person's life, robbing the person of truly living in the moment.

If a concern or worry is not a serious situation, it is important to learn to put it in the background. Mistakes are made by every person. If we are able to forgive others, it is important to also learn to give ourselves the same grace to make mistakes and be forgiven. The best way to do this is to keep busy and focused on life moving forward, reminding yourself that what cannot be changed can at least be *learned from*. Most times, if you are truly and effectively engaged in the present and in pursuing a life that is happy and productive, past mistakes will have little to no long-term effect.

2. Don't Sweat the Small Stuff.

Learn to deal with the minutiae that life throws at you. So many things happen that can throw us off balance. Discover ways to deal with distractions quickly and efficiently. Train yourself to recognize what is really a concern and what is just drama and details. Systematic scheduling of your time will help to alleviate many distractions and keep you moving forward despite your worries or insecurities.

3. Know Your Strengths and Weaknesses.

All people have areas in life where they shine and other areas that hold them back. Whether they be skillsets, physical advantages, or mental aptitude, any truly effective person is able to use these strengths to his or her advantage and avoid allowing weaknesses to slow progress down. Likewise, if a person is aware of his or her weaknesses, it is important to work on these things to continue developing and growing as a person. A weakness doesn't have to remain a weakness forever.

Revisit the ***Strengths and Weaknesses Survey*** in the Appendix to help better understand where your talents lie and try to use these approaches to support yourself and others around you.

4. Learn How You Learn.

It is vital to know which learning styles work best for you personally. Effective classroom teachers learn this about their students from the beginning and are better able to instruct them by using many different teaching styles. Some students are auditory learners, visual learners, tactile (kinesthetic) learners, or writing-dependent learners. Adults are no different, and the point of life is to engage in _continuous learning_. Do you learn better by listening to a verbal recording, reading a book (e.g., e-book or hard copy), or by taking notes while reading or listening to information? Some people adapt well to all of these styles, but it is important to discover what works best for you and continue engaging in learning about new things every day. With the internet at our fingertips, we can look up random questions and find information at virtually any time. It is a great idea to carry a book or e-book on the go, and also to look for opportunities to learn new skills from a bucket list (e.g., YouTube has instructional videos on just about every possible skill). There is an infinite volume of human knowledge that can be acquired if you place learning as a priority, and then determine the mechanism for information transfer that works best for you personally.

5. Face Your Fears.

If there is a situation or encounter that you are really nervous or concerned about, it can be debilitating. Here are some suggestions on how to face fears and successfully conquer them:

1. Understand the severity of the situation. Don't go "lion hunting with a BB gun."

2. Assess what you are trying to accomplish with any encounter before engaging in it.

3. Be prepared for different possible outcomes. Make sure the reward far outweighs the risk before engaging.

4. Consider involving someone who understands the situation.

5. Understand that it may take more than one encounter to overcome your fear.

6. Celebrate and enjoy the satisfaction of conquering fears. It feels pretty awesome!

(Author's Note: Fear has many faces and, as mentioned above, can be very debilitating. If you feel that your fears are causing serious issues of avoidance or withdrawal, don't hesitate to seek professional help so it doesn't hold you back on fully experiencing what life has to offer.)

6. Expose Yourself to Self-Help Materials.

There are myriad materials available that are helpful in positively directing thoughts and feelings. There is also a lot of advice on how to deal with people, situations, and most importantly, ourselves. These come in the form of books, videos, blogs, and speakers. Some gurus have been around for quite some time but are timeless in their advice, but there are also new sources of material each year.

(Author's note: Be cautious when choosing sources of self-help. If these conflict with your core beliefs, religion, or values, don't even consider them.)

7. Orient Yourself with a Verse or Quote of the Day.

Just spending a brief moment in the morning with a beverage of choice and a great motivational quote or saying can have a lasting effect as you navigate through your day. It can help focus you on self-improvement or start the day off with the right mindset. The quote could come from any source and can be related to many different topics. If you read it, internalize it, apply it to your day, and maybe even memorize it, you may get an unexpected boost of enthusiasm and productivity. You may also be less likely to react to external negativities. Plus, positivity tends to be catching to those around you!

Make sure you choose a source that is appropriate for you and is consistently uplifting.

8. Know and Understand Your Stressors.

Stressors are objects, persons, or situations that cause stress. It is vital to be aware of them so we can more easily deal with their effects. Unfortunately, the best way to know our stressors is to have experienced them. At some point we have two options. One is to take evasive action to avoid any contact. If this isn't possible, our other option is to develop a prepared response to the situation.

If a new situation arises and becomes stressful, it is a good idea to know how you best deal with stress generally. Below are general ways to keep stress under control:

1. Determine immediately if you or others are in danger. If you are, leave right away or take evasive action.

2. If leaving is not an option and you are not in danger, take a few seconds to analyze the situation.

3. Take a few deep, slow breaths.

4. Direct your focus toward something else, if possible.

5. Have a mantra prepared and memorized to say over and over during the contact.

6. Don't do anything that will further intensify the situation.

7. Reiterate to yourself that the situation is probably only temporary.

8. After it's over, consider discussing the situation and your reaction with a close friend or confidant.

In having an idea of what to say during a situation and a plan of how to react, it can allow a person to deescalate stress and make better decisions while in the moment.

9. Spend Quality Time with People in Other Age Groups.

Many of us feel much more comfortable with people our own age. This is understandable. Consider befriending people who are younger _and_ older. You will be surprised to find that many times they have different, but no less valuable, perspectives on life and how it should be approached. This can be quite refreshing to hear…and very eye-opening! Obtaining cross-generational knowledge allows a person to learn from those who are younger and older, for greater overall adaptability to the present and future. This includes addressing future retirement-related decisions and even the ever-evolving world of technology. Be prepared to take the role of learner or advisor in any relationship–and to constantly switch between these roles–to create deep abiding friendships.

10. Keep a Calendar and Make Entries…Even if You Are Not Busy.

Organize and plan your days consistently and you will soon experience the benefit of having your whole day prepared and ready for you to tackle. By using an electronic device, it is a very simple process. Even without a phone or tablet, it is easy to keep a printed calendar in a prominent place where you can note any plans or activities. It is a good idea to plan the next day the night before and make entries as they come up. Even if you have nothing planned for the next day, it is a good idea to review what you accomplished that day and make notes. This can help you set goals and finish projects in a timelier manner; it can also help ensure you don't forget upcoming appointments, deadlines, and events.

Keeping a calendar is a great way to make sure you did what you needed to do, and it should help you sleep better knowing you are prepared for the next day.

(Author's note: I personally keep my appointments on my phone and also keep a daily to-do list on my desk. My wife also keeps track of my appointments. She knows I'm forgetful!)

2. Examine the situation carefully to determine if you were possibly at fault in some way.

3. Address your feelings of resentment with a close friend or confidant.

4. Stay busy and don't let resentment take over the day, or any other extended period of time. Allow yourself a set amount of time to consider it and think through it, and then force yourself to think of other things. You may need to do this exercise for several days (or longer) until you are able to move past your feelings.

5. Discuss what happened with the other party involved at some point–if this is feasible.

6. Realize that true forgiveness doesn't happen overnight. It's usually a process.

7. Once you reconcile with a person, don't bring it up again–*ever*.

Forgetting is tough. Forgiveness is even tougher. When you are able to forget, forgiveness will probably follow. Don't let either hold you back from moving forward with your life!

13. Develop a Hobby that You Really Enjoy.

An enjoyable hobby can affect your life in so many ways. Just about anything can qualify as a hobby. The key is that you love it!

Here are some benefits of having a hobby:

1. It enhances the desire to learn and develop new ideas.

2. A hobby can fill a time void on some days...if there is such a thing.

3. It helps develop new friendships with those who have similar interests.

4. A hobby can distract a person from stress and life's daily irritations.

5. It helps a person diversify his or her approach to recreation.

6. It can help develop new partnerships and skillsets.

7. It can create travel opportunities.

8. A hobby can even evolve into a money-producing venture.

In Chapter Nine you will read more about how a purposeful hobby can breathe new life into anyone who is looking for a way to increase and enrich their daily life and experiences.

14. Drive Home Different Ways.

Getting into a rut is usually counterproductive. When we do the same old things the same old ways, we are in a rut. One of the best and most interesting ways to avoid this pattern is to vary your itinerary every time you travel to a destination that you frequently visit. The next time you go to the store, go the back way. The next time you drive home from work, take another route. The next time you visit your sibling, take the road less travelled. You will be surprised at what you discover and the people you will meet along the way.

15. Study and Internalize Your Religion and Spiritual Beliefs.

Many of us profess to be spiritual and members of a certain religion or denomination but have not taken the opportunity to dig deeper regarding the basis of what we are practicing. It's easy to go to a place of worship and just listen, but getting the most out of life requires that we put more effort into understanding our faith and its principles. Delving into the fundamentals of the belief system, its history, and the reasons for the traditions and teachings can be tremendously rewarding.

Becoming fully engaged in your religion and its beliefs can provide you with more guidance in your daily life, giving you greater confidence that you are on the right path. It can also help you understand the religious beliefs of those around you.

16. Project the Person You Wish to Be.

In order to develop a new mindset or to make changes in your personality, select a trait and act as though it is already a part of you. For example, if you want to be more confident, begin by projecting confidence in how you walk and speak (e.g., stand up straighter, look people in the eye, and project as you answer questions). Sometimes it helps to imagine yourself demonstrating and portraying the traits you wish to have so they feel more natural when you try them out in real life. If you want to be healthy, act as though you are healthy. If you want to make new friends, smile and be gregarious; welcoming traits draw friendships to a person.

It is important to remember that people treat us how we _allow them_ to treat us. We can train them to react differently by projecting the proper image. Sometimes it is easier to begin by picturing yourself with a new trait and roleplaying in the mirror. By planting these mental pictures, there's a likelihood that they will become part of your projected image. With positive feedback, these traits can become part of your psychological makeup and move you closer to becoming the person you desire to be.

17. Put Up a Bird Feeder...or Two or Three.

As simple as it may seem, bird feeders have proven to be a great psychological boost for people of all ages. The idea of attracting and helping nature's creatures is very appealing and also very rewarding. Many people watch for hours while the birds enjoy the well-placed food; some actually schedule a part of the day to watch. It is very relaxing. People find it fascinating to watch birds, as different as they are, interact with each other harmoniously. We could all learn from that.

(Author's note: Protect your bird feeders from squirrels!)

18. Be Competitive.

Competition takes on many forms. A person can be competitive in sports activities, in games such as cards, and in business settings; one can even be competitive against himself or herself (e.g., competing against a previous best time for running a mile). As a matter of fact, one can be competitive in almost anything.

Competition, for some, has a way of bringing out the best one has to offer. When striving to win, a person can become more focused, work harder, and not accept failure as readily. This can allow for high productivity and outstanding accomplishment.

For others, competition has a way of bringing out the worst. It can bring out a win-at-all-cost mentality. Those with uncontrolled tempers have a difficult time being involved in competitive situations.

Whichever category you belong, it is important to allow for these considerations:

1. Always put competition in perspective. If it involves your livelihood, take it more seriously. If it doesn't, be competitive but enjoy it.

2. Regardless of how important the competition is to you, it is also important to your competitor. Always show respect to your opponent.

3. If it's not a serious competition, attempt to adjust your competitive level to those involved.

4. If it is not serious, put restrictions on yourself to even things up skill wise. Sometimes this can provide an invaluable opportunity to encourage and build another person's self-esteem and inner drive.

5. Never let a weaker opponent know, or even suspect, you are not competing at your best, as this can be insulting.

6. Regardless of the competition and the stakes, be a good loser and a gracious winner.

19. Raise a Pet.

Obtaining and raising a pet is a most rewarding endeavor. In doing so, you are not only taking care of a beloved animal, you are also building and exercising feelings of self-worth and empathy. The time and effort you expend to care for the pet enables you to move the focus from you and put it on a creature that really needs you.

If you are thinking about raising a pet, these considerations are so important:

1. Make sure you have the time and wherewithal to furnish it with a good home. Be aware of the longevity of the pet, and ensure you are prepared to care for it for the full duration of its life.

2. Do your research about what pet would be the best match for you. If you're not sure, pet sitting is a great way to get to know different species and breeds.

3. Make sure your whole family is on board with bringing a pet into your lives. Be prepared to be the sole caregiver for your new pet regardless of whether it was your idea or not.

4. Know your community, apartment, or rental rules concerning pets.

5. Consider putting the pet through a training program.

6. Protect the pet from disease, temperature extremes, danger, predators, and parasites to the greatest degree possible.

7. Find out if there are any environmental dangers for your new pet (e.g., some landscaping plants are toxic to dogs).

8. Make your home pet-proof.

9. Do not consider having a domesticated pet if you envision tying it up or housing it in the backyard for any period of time.

20. Avoid Decision Constipation.

Don't be one of those people who anguishes over small, inconsequential decisions. Some people expend valuable time making decisions that really aren't that important. If this describes you, follow these guidelines:

1. Categorize decisions on a one to five scale, with five being the most consequential.

2. On less consequential decisions, give yourself a time limit to come to a conclusion.

3. For more consequential decisions, spend more time researching the options. Give yourself a time limit in these situations as well.

4. Solicit help from others but ultimately depend on your gut feeling. If a decision involves others, you may want to consult with them.

5. Make a pros and cons list to help you decide.

(Author's Note: There are times when it's impossible to know the right decision. Sometimes, you just have to make the best decision, and then make it right).

21. Select and Denote ICE Numbers in Your Phone.

In Case of Emergency, or ICE, numbers are the phone numbers for those you wish contacted immediately. When coming across a person in peril, a first responder will check the person's phone to try to locate those who need to be notified right away.

In your contacts, list these individuals as ICE and enter their names alongside. It is suggested to list at least two or three ICE numbers. Knowing that the right person will be contacted provides security and peace of mind. Hopefully, these won't be needed, but you never know!

(Author's note: There are phone apps available that will not only contact your emergency numbers, but also store pertinent medical information such as allergies and medications in case this is ever needed.)

22. Get Involved Politically.

What an opportunity! Getting involved at any level politically can really ramp up enthusiasm and get you plugged into the world around you! Imagine the impact you can have on many lives, not only close by, but even nationally and worldwide. It is also a way to meet new people, learn new things, and engage with others about how to best develop and support your community.

There are so many opportunities to become politically engaged. The important thing is to make sure you strongly believe in the person or cause that you throw support behind. If you do it half-heartedly, it will be obvious, and what should be a fun experience will end up as a chore.

Here are some suggestions:

1. Support and campaign for a local candidate in your hometown, county, district, or state. You can do this by volunteering to put up signs, knock on doors and talk with people, set up and host functions, or manage the phones at the campaign headquarters.

2. Help to advance a certain political party and its agenda.

3. Know and understand your core beliefs as they align with a given platform and "sing these to the world."

4. Become involved in national elections. (A person can start by getting involved at the local level.)

5. Become a poll worker.

6. Become a candidate yourself. If you see change that needs to happen, step up to the plate!

Becoming involved in shaping the world, or at least your small part of it, is one of the most gratifying ways to can serve your fellow man and also discover, develop, and nurture your own personal beliefs.

23. Keep a Diary or Journal.

Keeping a diary or journal and making consistent entries can be a blessing, not only to you but also to those close to you. It is a great tool for reminiscing about your past and for keeping track of what happens in your life. Journaling can allow for increased introspection. This enables us to better understand the choices we make and why we make them, assess mistakes and successes for learning opportunities, and monitor our personal growth and development. Journals can also assist with accountability when setting personal goals.

Many who just lost a parent or grandparent have remarked that they wished they had spent more intimate time with the person, asking questions to find out more about the relative's life. By keeping a diary, you can at least furnish a glimpse of your life for your loved ones to cherish.

These suggestions can help you to begin journaling in a meaningful way:

1. Diaries and journals can be done electronically, but those that are handwritten are better received and enjoyed.

2. Make entries consistently, like once a week, once a day, or at the end of each month. The more often you make entries, the more accurate they will be. Details tend to fade very quickly.

3. Record not only happenings, but also feelings.

4. Don't shy away from entering negative situations. Those close to you will appreciate knowing how you felt and reacted to various challenges.

5. Include photos, travel stickers, and other mementos related to entries.

6. Always date each entry. You can even include the approximate time of day for each.

7. Keep your diary in a handy place so that you can easily make entries and, if anything happens to you, it will be easy for others to locate.

8. When you are feeling down, use writing as a pick-me-up.

9. Consider stating, tracking, and highlighting goals and accomplishments, keeping track of obstacles and challenges faced.

10. Include a picture of yourself and/or your family on an annual basis.

(Author's Note: It can be said that a diary is a gift that keeps on giving.)

24. Be on Time and Start on Time.

One of the best ways to feel in control of your life is to make a commitment to yourself that you will always **be on time**. Implicit in that statement that is that anything you are in charge of will **start on time** and **end on time**. We all know people who are perpetually late; it's a bad habit and can tarnish a reputation because it can come across as rude and inconsiderate. If there is ever a chance you are going to be late for an appointment, it is important to contact the other party and let him or her know. Even if you actually make it on time, the person will absolutely appreciate the courtesy.

25. Use Your Cell Phone for Communication Only.

Cell phones are one of our biggest blessings–AND biggest curses. Because of them, we are able to stay in touch with practically anyone in the world, at practically any time. We also have access to almost anything we need or want to know.

This comes at a price.

Even though our phones make communication easy and readily available, it also increases interruptions and distractions to the point of being a major problem.

One or more of these suggestions may be just what you need to put _you_ back in control of your cell phone:

1. Set your phone up to use it only for talking and texting.

2. Relegate email, social media, and search capabilities to another device and use these applications selectivity.

3. Have a set schedule for checking email and perusing social media, rather than doing it several times throughout the day.

4. Keep reminders and signals just loud enough that they do not disturb those around you. (They can also drive you crazy!)

5. Keep your phone in your pocket or in a purse when in the company of others. Don't answer other calls while engaged with someone else.

6. Always use Bluetooth connectivity in your vehicle (if available) while driving and abide by local laws (as applicable).

7. Do not allow cell phone usage at the dinner table.

8. If at all possible, leave your phone in another room when sleeping.

With that being said...

Fortunately, or unfortunately, our cell phones are our lifelines today. We depend on them for so many things. It's up to you to decide how best to utilize it in your work-a-day world. The trick is to make sure it's not a distraction that keeps you from engaging in relationships or causes you to miss out on life's real-time adventures.

26. Embrace the Journey.

There are many journeys in life. Some are very positive and lead to great things; others are perilous, leading to challenges that make us question why.

There are many people who are "completion oriented," a term commonly used to describe a person who believes the only important part of a journey is the end of it. While finishing projects and completing goals are obviously important, there are many lessons and blessings that can be gained by embracing, accepting, and enjoying the process and journey.

You should approach each part of life with the outlook that you will be a better person because you took a given path, and then be open to new things along the way. This perspective and positive attitude can be life changing.

27. Pay It Forward.

Many times, people will do something great for us but, for whatever reason, we cannot pay them back. They may even refuse to let you reciprocate. Don't worry. The next time someone else needs help, take advantage of the opportunity to *pay it forward*. You will be a blessing to another person and feel blessed in the process. Never underestimate how wonderful it can feel to do something nice for another person–even anonymously–and *especially* if you are feeling low personally at the time. Knowing the effect you have had on another person's day, week, or life can make these little activities become an addiction!

As suggested in Chapter Six, "Be the most generous person you know!"

28. Sometimes Things Have to Get Worse Before They Can Get Better.

Life doesn't always improve on an upswing; many times, we have to step back in order to move forward. Understand and accept this fact and you will be in better control of how your future plays out.

29. Don't Take Yourself Too Seriously.

We all screw up. We all do great things. We all second guess ourselves. And we all know that, if we could do some things over again, we would probably jump at the chance. It's all a part of life. It's all part of our psychological makeup.

Here are some great suggestions for how to stop second-guessing your life and feel more comfortable with who you are:

1. If you wronged someone, apologize and make it right–whatever it takes.

2. If you made a bad decision and it can be corrected, figure out what it would take and follow through on it. Don't continually beat yourself up over it.

3. If you made a bad decision and it cannot be corrected, do whatever you can to offset the damage. Learn to live with the results and help others adjust. Again, don't continually beat yourself up.

4. If you made a great decision, "pat yourself on the back" and move on. Don't gloat for long–and do so in private!

5. If someone took advantage of you, let the person know you are aware of it and ask him or her to rectify the situation. Whatever the outcome, move on as soon as possible and use the knowledge gained to guide your future encounters.

6. Never underestimate your importance in others' lives. In the same vein, don't overestimate your importance.

7. Learn to laugh at yourself when you do something ridiculous.

Always remember that each decision you have made in your life has led to challenges and windfalls. To erase a bad part would most certainly detract from the things you hold dear–such as your relationships and children, or opportunities that have shaped who you are. Our lives are a rich fabric of events, with each contributing to the quilt we become. Everything happens for a reason.

30. Be Your Own Best Friend.

It's been said that "if you can't love yourself, you can't truly love anyone else." The reasoning behind this is that without truly learning to love who you are and recognizing your personal worth in this world, you have nothing to compare love to.

Many people misinterpret 'loving yourself' by comparing it to conceit and a warped opinion of self-worth. We all have met people who walk into a room with the attitude that the party can now begin because they *have arrived*. These people probably have very low self-esteem and, for whatever reason, feel a need to overcompensate.

If a person truly learns to love and appreciate himself or herself as a person, it is evident in the individual's manner and confidence; it becomes clear that the individual is content in his or her character and value and doesn't feel a need to prove it to others. This type of person knows he or she can affect the world, but the world does not owe homage in return. Self-confidence allows a person to feel in control of life and provides the wherewithal to deal with any challenges or situations that come along. Such a person acknowledges that there will be others who attempt 'to rain on the parade,' but getting a bit damp doesn't stop a person from living life to the fullest.

31. It's Never Too Late.

There are so many examples of people who accomplished great things at an advanced age. If there is something you want to do, ***do it***. Regardless of age, adopt a "go for it" attitude. You just may become one of those people who achieves great things, even though the odds were stacked against you. Similarly, though you may not achieve legendary acclaim for your efforts, you are likely to be a hero to those around you who admire your courage and determination.

In Conclusion:

We don't live in a perfect world, and none of us are perfect people. Many things can happen over the years that make us believe we are not worthy of the lives we have, or lead us to pick apart our decisions, blaming ourselves or carrying anger for various outcomes. The good news is that we have the capacity to control these thoughts so they don't have to drag us down to mediocrity.

If you are having serious concerns, and these concerns are affecting the very essence of who you are–or impeding your happiness and fulfillment–don't hesitate to seek professional help. There is no stigma attached to finding a great counsellor with whom you can share your worries and challenges. Sometimes an outside perspective is exactly what is needed to reposition the angle through which we are looking at life.

You can also take steps toward gaining control of your personal life, such as training yourself to focus on what's most important, controlling your attitude toward yourself and your surroundings, and being prepared for life's twists and turns. These are just a few steps that can be taken to get you on the road to becoming the person you've always wanted to be.

"The ONLY important reason to look back is to see how far you've come."
–KIA Automobile Advertisement

CHAPTER EIGHT

APPEARANCE STRATEGIES

"A great appearance is fleeting, so do what you can to make it the best you can, for as long as you can. You will be surprised and amazed by its impact on your life."

–Author

Let's be honest. Many (if not most) people spend a lot of time, effort, and money to look more attractive. They feel better when they look better. Many people relate to and interact more with others when they believe that they look their best. They feel more confident and believe they can be more successful with a sharp appearance.

Others say that too much emphasis is placed on looks, and it's a waste of time, energy, and resources to attempt to improve appearance. There isn't a right or a wrong answer necessarily, as what a person feels about himself or herself is actually in the driver's seat. Oftentimes, how a person perceives his or her appearance can impact the desire to engage with others, socialize, move confidently, and take risks that lead to rewards and new opportunities. A person's self-perception can indeed assist or impede life.

The purpose of this chapter is to provide some helpful and effective strategies for those in the first group–those who wish to improve their lives and feel that a positive self-image can certainly help. Life coaches often help individuals improve self-image and personal appearance to attain more confidence and success, referring to this as "developing a personal brand." For a person at any age, we can develop and build on assets, making small changes that help us feel more comfortable and confident in our interactions.

As most of us find out, changes in appearance are usually very subtle and take place over a long period of time. Maybe this is a blessing, but we need to understand that it is easier and much more effective to deal with these changes sooner, rather than later.

Please don't misunderstand: Physical changes are not necessarily bad, or even inevitable. Realize that if there are aspects of your appearance you are not pleased with, there may be steps you can take to alter them, or at least make them less concerning to you. Will some of them come under the heading of "vanity?" Maybe. That's OK. If, somehow, it makes you feel better about yourself to work on these issues–go for it.

When you go through this list of strategies, note the ones you want to incorporate right away. There may be a few. Do understand, however, that many strategies may apply to changes that could affect your appearance down the road. Even though some may seem they would never apply, you may be surprised. Age, time, and life's changes can add some twists!

(Author's note: As important as your appearance is for self-esteem and feeling confident, it is important to refrain from making it a focal point in life. Take necessary and practical steps to make these strategies successful, do your research, monitor the results for effectiveness, and enjoy the process. If you keep it all in perspective, you will, over the years, reap the benefits of spending a little time, effort, and resources to make you–a better looking and more confident you).

1. Take the Paper Bag Test.

If you want to form an unbiased opinion of your body and where it needs to be improved, get a paper bag from your local store and cut out holes for your eyes. Now strip down to nothing *(Author's note: You may want to do this in private!),* put the bag over your head, and check yourself out in front of a full-length mirror–back and front.

Why the paper bag? We all have a tendency to have slanted opinions of ourselves, and especially of our bodies. Men normally overlook obvious flaws while women are usually very critical of what they see. The paper bag is supposed to make your judgment more objective. Checking yourself out in this way will help you decide where you need to focus your efforts for improvement.

This is actually a fun exercise. You may find yourself chuckling and laughing, but you will also form a more accurate opinion of your body's flaws and assets, which will help you with your motivation to improve!

2. Work on Your Posture.

Ever notice how many people walk stooped over and slouching? This is even an issue for young adults! It makes a person appear older and can eventually become problematic to health, if continued. It can cause back problems, a permanently slouched posture, and reduced strength. Just adjusting your posture increases lung capacity and can reduce shoulder and back pain. Aside from the potential for medical concerns, sitting with proper posture and standing up straight lengthens the body and places a person's figure and form at its best. It also helps a person to be more self-aware and alert. This is one of the reason phrases such as "sit-up and take notice" and "stand at attention" are common, indicating the pairing of mental and physical acuity.

There are many causes for slouching. Sitting is a major contributor to slouching and stooping. Think about how much time you actually spend in a seated position (e.g., when driving, at computer or desk, during meals, and while relaxing). People often are not aware of poor postural habits when seated during these activities. This can lead to lowered core muscle strength and, eventually, a stooping shape that can become permanent over the years.

Another big cause of poor posture is constant phone usage. When you consider how much people use phones for talking, texting, reading, and searching, we spend a lot of time with our heads down and backs bent into a kyphotic posture (rounded back).

It is also important to consider some health reasons that could cause postural problems such as advancing spinal dysfunction, osteoporosis, joint degeneration, respiratory problems, and high blood pressure. For this reason, a person should be checked at least yearly for any of these physical challenges. For those who do not have underlying medical conditions, here is a list of adjustments that can ease problems associated with bad posture:

1. Lose weight if this is needed. Extra weight around the midsection can pull the pelvis forward taking the spine out of alignment and adding stress to the lower back.

2. Wear supportive, correctly fitting bras. An unsupportive bra can affect the curve of the spine, lead to upper back problems and pinched nerves, and cause a person to slouch.

3. Ramp up an exercise program to include more walking and weight-bearing exercises.

4. Ditch the high heels as much as possible.

5. Look up and out while standing, walking, or running.

6. Press the tops of the shoulders back, like a person standing at attention in the military.

7. Don't sit on a wallet.

8. Wear correctly fitting shoes and replace them when needed.

9. Sit up straight while reclining and don't cross the legs for extended periods of time.

10. Learn and perform daily stretches designed to increase flexibility and strengthen core and back muscles.

11. Use an inversion table, as mentioned in Chapter Four.

Poor posture makes a person look old, even if he or she is not, so it is important to do what can be done to improve it. If a person is consistent, improvement happens fairly quickly, including decreased pain and better self-image—as well as improved overall appearance.

3. Accept Your Height—Its Advantages and Disadvantages.

There is so much discussion about height. Some is positive. Some is negative. Really tall people want to be shorter. Short people want to be taller. Rather than discuss the pros and cons of being any given height, let's review some strategies a person can use if he or she is bothered by a lack of height:

1. Wear shoes with a heel. These come in varying heights.

2. Wear shoes that have a lift built in.

3. Select clothes with lengthwise patterns rather than horizontal patterns, as horizontal stripes and patterns can make a person appear stockier.

4. Alter a hairstyle so it's not as flat to the crown of the head.

5. Make sure clothing fits properly. Hem pants to the proper length for a sharp, tailored appearance.

6. Wear a hat as part of each outfit and adopt this as a personal style preference.

7. Hang out with people closer to your height.

8. Stand up straight–do not slouch.

9. Try not to overcompensate by using a louder voice or adopting an overbearing personality. These make others jump to unflattering clichés and stereotypes.

Conversely, if you are very tall...

1. Don't slouch to minimize yourself. It won't make you shorter, but it will make you appear less confident.

2. Hang out with people who are closer to your height.

3. Avoid purchasing a compact car. Aside from the jokes you will be forced to endure, there is a higher chance

of blood clots and deep vein thrombosis (DVT) when driving long distances if a person is unable to stretch out.

4. For the same reasons indicated above, consider upgraded seating on airplanes, and take frequent stretch breaks during long flights.

5. Avoid wearing heels or boots that are so tall that they take the emphasis off your smile and shift it to your height.

6. Especially if you are male, watch your body language and be aware of the size difference between you and others. Simple gestures and hand expressions can seem more intimidating when a person is much larger proportionally, especially for women and children. This is especially important in a professional setting.

7. Make sure your clothing fits. Make sure shirts remain tucked in, find pants long enough to be hemmed to the correct length, and select dresses that cover all the important assets (particularly when leaning or bending over).

A wise person once said, 'Height has nothing to do with stature.' Regardless of your height, this is a great approach to living and loving yourself as you are!

4. Flatten Your Tummy without Sit-Ups and Crunches.

There is no better way to flatten your stomach than taking part in a consistent exercise program, but there is a tip you can use to make your midsection look much trimmer. It's simple and easy. All you have to do is suck your abdominal muscles in and hold them for approximately 20-30 seconds and do it about 10 or so times a day–that's it!

While this activity will never replace a good core exercise regimen, it really does help with posture, as well as overall confidence and appearance. Plus, you will probably have a good time doing it!

My advice is to try to make it fun: Pick out a time or choose a particular situation when you will do this activity so that you are consistent.

(Author's note: One friend does this activity whenever he sees a red traffic light. Another does it at the top of each hour. I do it whenever I see a person who, ahem...needs to do it also.)

5. Try These Tricks to Combat Turkey Neck.

Turkey neck occurs when skin loses elasticity and when muscle tone is lost, causing the skin under the chin to sag. There are different degrees of turkey neck and it can be a progressive problem.

There are some non-surgical tricks that can be done to alleviate this appearance problem. It is important to start them early, but they are effective at any age. If this is a problem you are dealing with (or don't want to have to deal with in the future), try these simple suggestions:

1. Keep your head up. This will help keep the skin from becoming loose.

2. Moisturize your skin nightly.

3. Sleep on your back with only one pillow. This keeps the skin taut for a longer period of time. You can also use a contour pillow for the same purpose.

4. Use the Butterfly Exercise. Apply moisturizer to your neck and fingertips, cross your hands like you are choking yourself. With your fingers push the skin outward and hold. Performing this exercise for five minutes on most days will definitely bring improvement. You can also do the same basic movement using only one hand.

5. Put your head back as far as you can and imitate an exaggerated chewing motion with your jaw for 20 seconds at a time, twice a day.

6. Put your head back and "kiss the ceiling" with your lips for about 20 seconds, twice a day.

7. Chew gum, as this allows for exercise of the jaw and neck musculature.

8. Watch your phone use. Time spent looking down at a cell phone makes this situation worse, along with your posture.

There are devices designed to massage and tighten skin. Some claim to be pretty effective, but these are usually expensive as well. There are surgical procedures to consider also. But, if you follow these quick and easy tricks, you will definitely see marked improvement. The goal is to start early and be consistent!

6. Bring Your Eyewear up to the 21st Century.

Nothing screams "old" more than outdated eyewear. It's not unusual to see people who haven't changed their frame style for 5, 10, or even 20 years. By that time, a pair of glasses is going to make a person look dated.

When you are out and about, check out the styles that others are wearing so that when you visit an eyecare specialist, you have a good idea of what's in, and what's not. They are usually up on the latest styles and can help you make a decision that will keep you fashionable.

7. Drink Enough Water.

We discussed water consumption in Chapter Four, but water has other benefits for the appearance. There is a lot of conjecture about how much water one should drink daily, but there is no denying that drinking an adequate amount has a profound effect on the look of a person's skin and hair. It helps to moisturize the skin, reduce the effects of rosacea and acne, and aid in wrinkle prevention. It also helps by strengthening hair follicles, promoting healthy, attractive hair growth and preventing dandruff.

8. Keep Your Teeth Beautiful and Healthy.

Teeth are one of the first things many people notice about a person. Every day we meet people whose teeth are discolored, chipped, broken and even missing. There are many, even those of comfortable means, who don't place oral hygiene as a priority. This is a serious mistake. Not only does it detract from their over-all appearance, it can also lead to more serious health problems.

The following are a few precautions that can be taken to prevent dental problems from becoming a distraction from your appearance:

1. If you consume coffee, tea, or other foods that stain the teeth, brush (or at least rinse) right after consumption.

2. Floss every night.

3. Consider having your teeth whitened if you have heavy staining. There are many affordable products and procedures offered.

4. Immediately replace or repair any teeth that are chipped, missing, or broken, as these can result in further health complications if left untreated.

5. Brush at least twice a day to remove plaque and have your teeth professionally cleaned at least twice a year.

6. Stimulate your gums by brushing and massaging.

7. If you need braces, get them. There are invisible (or less visible) progressive options that can be used in adults to reduce a person's insecurity about having braces at a more mature age.

8. Combine a visit to the dentist with one of the cleaning sessions. Even if there are no obvious problems, there could be some hidden issues.

9. Address any issues right away. Don't put them off.

There is no excuse for letting your teeth become a detriment to your appearance and health. Dentistry has made great improvements over the years and is more reasonably priced than ever before. Make sure your dentist is on your trusted vendor list and don't be afraid to ask questions.

9. Use Your Best Side When Taking Pictures.

In an age of social media, good pictures are a must. We want to always put our best foot forward and look as good as possible, for obvious reasons. Knowing how to take a good picture of yourself can reduce anxiety over being photographed. It can also increase your satisfaction in looking back at snapshots of beautiful memories, allowing you to be less critical of your appearance and just enjoy reminiscing. Before taking pictures, consider these strategies:

1. Check yourself out in a mirror to see which is your best side. We look different from different angles, so figure out which one is best and use it as much as you can.

2. Take several pictures at a time and go back later to choose the best one for the occasion. With digital cameras, there's no reason to feel inhibited about the number of photos taken.

3. Decide the best distance from which to take selfies. Distance helps to eliminate and minimize flaws!

4. Suck your tummy in, especially for full-length pictures. It makes you look trimmer and helps you to stand up straight.

5. Consider using a prop if appropriate. Use your imagination to choose props for photos.

6. Use a real smile for a great shot.

7. Take advantage of photoshop and editing features, but don't overdo it.

8. Avoid extreme close-ups. When streaming, video conferencing, or using FaceTime, stay as far back from the camera as you possibly can while still communicating effectively.

Photos are ubiquitous. It is important to feel good about the pictures we take–and take the best pictures we can–as people often use these to make decisions about us, sometimes even before they meet us.

10. Drive a Vehicle that Projects the Image You Want to Convey.

Your choice of what you drive is important. Different vehicles say different things. You can exude success by driving a luxury car. You can ooze coolness by driving a sports car. You can appear macho by showing up in a 4 x 4 truck. Whatever image you want to portray can be expressed by your transportation.

With that being said…

The most important consideration regarding your vehicle is that it must be affordable and reliable, particularly based on the discussion in Chapter Six. Aside from this, it should be kept neat and clean on the inside and outside. These are actually essential considerations, as people often transfer these characteristics to you, your work ethic, and your character, upon your first meeting.

(Author's note: One of my closest friends is an ultra-successful real estate agent and he drives a four-year-old mid-level sedan. Works for him!)

11. Work on This Muscle Group.

When people are asked the question: "What is the most important muscle group for good appearance?" The answer is always the same: the abdominal muscles. Flabby abs are a turn off for many people. The unfortunate thing is that even if they are covered up, people can usually still tell.

Keep this in mind and read more in Chapter Ten about how to change that chunky middle into your best physical asset.

12. Don't Wear Your Phone.

Clip-on belt cases are so out of style. They make a person look old and dated. If you carry a phone, and most of us do, put it in a pocket, out of sight, or in a purse. On a similar note, if you constantly carry a phone in your hand, you will appear unapproachable. Put your phone away when it is not in use!

13. Baby Your Skin.

Since we already addressed skin care in Chapter Four, we will discuss skin from an appearance standpoint in this chapter. There are so many things that can be done to protect your skin and, in essence, keep you looking younger and healthier. The catch is that they need to be started early and before the signs of aging become noticeable.

We've all seen a "beach freak" who is so tanned that the skin looks like a prune. This did not happen overnight. It is caused by many years of overexposure to the sun. The most important thing a person can do to prevent this is to apply a product with sunscreen anytime when going out into the sunlight. That's right–*anytime.* The key is to make it part of your routine. It doesn't take long to apply and should be done repeatedly for extended exposure.

Here are some additional strategies:

1. Start caring for your skin early.

2. Use a moisturizing lotion all over after showering. Pat down (don't wipe down) after showering and apply it while the skin is still moist. Pay particular attention to problem areas. (You know where they are.)

3. Drink enough water. (You've heard this already!)

4. Don't use soaps that dry out the skin.

5. Shower in lukewarm water, not hot.

On this same train of thought…

Two of the most obvious signs of aging, as mentioned before, are the skin of the neck and hands. Pay extra attention to these areas and you will be surprised how great they can look, even in your senior years.

14. Diminish Arm Bruising.

If you have it, you know what I'm talking about, and you hate it. If you don't have it, trust that you probably will at some point.

What causes us to bruise so easily? The main problem is that, as we age, our skin becomes thinner and we lose some of the protective fatty layer that cushions our blood vessels, making us more susceptible to bruising. In addition, sun exposure over the years causes skin to become brittle and thus more prone to bruising and tearing.

What can be done? Honestly, not much. There are over-the-counter medications available to speed up recovery that have mediocre results. Prevention is the most effective measure. Sunscreen and moisturizer applied regularly, as discussed above, are great preventatives, as is wearing protective elbow-length gloves while doing household or yard-related tasks.

If you are one of the lucky ones and it never becomes a problem, you should count your blessings.

15. Manage Man Boobs.

Man boobs, referred to medically as gynecomastia, are caused by the development of excess fat or breast tissue in men. This can be an extremely embarrassing issue for many men. There are even some health issues linked to excessive breast tissue growth in men. First let's look at the causes, and then a few ways to deal with this issue.

One of the most common causes of gynecomastia is hormone fluctuations. This is usually the result of age, obesity, excessive alcohol consumption, or lack of exercise. Many of these issues actually act to exacerbate other health concerns. For example, excess alcohol consumption can cause weight gain, and fat tissue produces estrogen, a female hormone. All individuals (female and male) have a bit of estrogen, but when testosterone-to-estrogen ratios change significantly, this can cause breast tissue development. For some, extra estrogen can throw hormonal controls out of balance and can lead to further stress, which is then accompanied by more alcohol consumption and weight gain, creating a vicious cycle. Many times, the fix starts with changing habits.

So, what needs to be done? It is important to check with your trusted medical advisor to see if you have any underlying health issues that could be the cause. This usually involves a simple blood test. The next step is to join a gym and schedule a few sessions with a trusted fitness trainer. One of the most important steps is to adjust your diet by eliminating (or severely limiting) alcohol, consuming more lean protein, and allowing for few, if any, starches in the diet (e.g., bread, pasta, potatoes).

Because men have a tendency to lose testosterone as they age, it may be an option to take medications that can alter or slow this loss. Because hormones must be carefully managed to reduce the chance of heart disease or other complications, a person should always check with a trusted medical advisor before *ever* considering the use of any hormonal agent.

While a person won't lose man boobs overnight, taking steps to get rid of them can have many added benefits in long-term overall health.

16. Be Wary of Fashion Fads but Have Some Fun!

Fashion rules change. One year you are supposed to wear leggings or tight jeans, and the next year the designers say baggy is in. How do you figure out what you should be wearing and what is just a fad? It's totally up to you! With that being said, you don't want to be wearing clothes that are sadly out of style. It is important to stay appropriate and relevant.

Here are some ideas to help you stay "with it:"

1. Make quality selections. You get what you pay for, and good clothes usually stay in style longer.

2. Always wear clothes that fit well.

3. Dress appropriately for the occasion. If you are under or overdressed, you will look out of place.

4. If it's not comfortable, don't wear it–and don't buy it.

5. When shopping, don't go directly to your favorite department. Check in other areas that feature different styles and look at how the clothes are paired on mannequins.

6. Check your closet out every year or so and get rid of clothes you haven't worn for a long time. You haven't worn them for a reason. Chances are they are probably out of style.

7. Try not to mix different styles (e.g., don't wear athletic shoes with a dress).

8. Stay as current as possible–but remember, you're not
    16 years old anymore!

Classic styles and colors stay hip for longer. Pairing khakis with a dress shirt has been in style for decades–and will likely be in style for decades longer. For ladies, a simple navy pencil skirt and white blouse can be accented with fashionable accessories while keeping the basic "canvas" both traditional and versatile. Having a core of traditional classics can allow a person to make small excursions into the fashion fray through accessories without overhauling a wardrobe (and budget) with each change in season and style.

17. Hide Your Physical Flaws.

We all have flaws. They are usually the first thing we notice when we look in the mirror, and they often have a tendency to irritate us.

So, what do we do? Well, we could ignore them. We could let them incessantly bug us. Or, we can make them less of an issue by hiding them.

One of the easiest ways to minimize flaws is to use fashion choices and clothing cut to cover them up. For example, if you're overweight, wear your shirttails out and wear loose pants that don't accentuate the waistline. If you're balding, wear a hat. If you're skinny, wear clothes with bold patterns and don't bare your arms. If you have big ears, wear your hair longer. You get the picture.

These are the types of things we shouldn't hesitate to ask friends for help with. Also, when shopping, it can be helpful to spend time with a fashion coordinator who is trained to get the most out of clothing options and variety. Most high-end fashion stores have these individuals on staff, and people should take advantage of their knowledge and experience!

18. Consider Tattoos Carefully.

If you already have tattoos that you regret, you have two basic choices. The first is to accept them as you have for years. The second is to have them removed, although that's not always easy. Tattoo removal is an expensive process and its success varies depending on the intensity of the ink, the skill of the artist, and the doctor doing the removal.

If you don't have any tattoos, you also have choices. The first is to avoid the temptation entirely. The second is, if you decide to get tattooed, consider where you place the item, as well as who will see it. Let these criteria be your guide.

In the younger years, tattoos are often a novelty. Individuals may get them without considering the long-term effects on others' perceptions. Different groups are more accepting, as well as different areas of the world. For this reason, if a person is still working, he or she should consider what a given industry or business profession considers appropriate, and whether he or she will be required to cover any exposed area that has been tattooed. Based on the dress code for some careers, a tattoo can lock a person into a lifetime of long sleeves, high collars, and long pants regardless of the climate–or the practicality and comfort of this attire while doing the job.

Many people today choose to express themselves with tattoos, commemorating people and things in their lives that hold great meaning. If you would like to do so and you have any hesitation of how it may potentially impact a future job, relationship, or business transaction, it is important to be as discreet as possible and place the tattoo in an area that can be covered up, just in case.

19. Care for Your Fingernails.

Clean, neat fingernails are an asset to anyone's appearance; the reverse can really detract from a person's image. People notice nails. They notice when you point, when you shake hands, and when you eat or drive. Their cleanliness and care represent your overall personal hygiene.

Some guys have a tendency to neglect their nails; some forget their existence entirely. Some women can go over the top with artificial talons. Here are some tips for having acceptable nails that do not detract from your overall look:

1. **Do not chew them!** The germs and grime that exist under the fingernails rivals some of our most filthy body parts.

2. Keep them trimmed so they don't get in the way of productivity.

3. If one becomes jagged, file it until it is smooth again.

4. If they get dirty, clean them, and use a nail brush or pick if needed.

5. Keep the cuticle pushed back or trimmed, as needed.

6. Wear gloves when performing tasks that could mess them up or stain them.

7. Apply a low gloss polish every so often. This tip is even for the guys. It helps to protect the nails and keep them looking clean and healthy.

8. If you see any abnormalities, get these checked out by a trusted medical advisor who specializes in hand care. These could be an indication of a more serious health problem.

20. Take Care of Your Hair.

If you are one of the lucky males who still has a full head of hair, take care of it! There are so many things that can and should be done to make hair last longer and look better. Healthy, shiny and youthful-looking hair is a blessing as a person gets older. These suggestions can help a person keep his or her hair looking its best:

1. Don't wash your hair unless it needs it. This strips the natural oils from it and makes it frizzy and coarse.

2. Rotate types of shampoos. Use one for oily hair, one
    for dry hair, one to increase body, and one to mend
    split ends, even if none of these situations is a
    problem. You may even want to add a coloring
    shampoo to the rotation, and follow the directions
    carefully. Use a conditioner also.

3. Don't use extremely stiff hairbrushes.

4. Use the warm or cool setting on the hairdryer. Heat
    can dry and damage hair.

5. If using color, it's best to use products that produce
    gradual change.

6. Alter your hairstyle every so often.

7. Keep a regular hair appointment with a trusted hair
    stylist or barber. This individual can offer great advice
    and also monitor any changes in your hair quality. Be
    receptive to suggestions if your hairstyle is becoming
    dated.

8. Rarely wear a hat or other head covering.

9. Use hair products that protect your hair from sun
    exposure. As with heat, the sun can damage hair and
    change its color.

10. Use a silk pillowcase for sleeping.

11. If a person is losing his or her hair, it is important to
    seek assistance rather than using radical styles to hide

the loss. Early intervention can stop or reverse some of the causes for hair loss.

12. Consider talking to a healthcare provider about vitamin supplementation if there are relatively rapid changes in hair texture, fullness, or color. Sometimes, this can be the result of a medical condition such as a thyroid disorder, an autoimmune condition, or a poor diet.

If you start early enough, haircare is a lot easier. Be prepared to spend a little bit more on good products. The difference in quality and effectiveness is well worth the added expense.

21. Manscape Beards and Mustaches.

Beards and mustaches are very popular, now especially, and are grown in many styles. If you decide to grow one, make sure the style fits your face.

If you are still in the professional work-a-day world, you should consider keeping facial hair close and tidy. If you decide to color it, make sure the dye matches head hair and is not too dark. Gray or white facial hair has a tendency to make a person appear older, so this should be considered before growing a new look. Additionally, growing facial hair to a length that is able to be shaped into the preferred style can take several days, so it is often preferable to try a new look during some time off so as to avoid the "scruffy stage" while getting started.

22. Eradicate Unwanted Hair.

Hair pops up in the craziest places! Among these locations are the ears, nose, back, neck, and other not-so-favored places on the face. It's a problem that is easy to take care of, but you have to monitor them closely, as they seem to pop up overnight. There are many tools available today to cut or remove unsightly follicle growth. You just need to take the time to do it. In your arsenal, you should have (at minimum) a 10x lighted mirror for the best accuracy in your attack.

(Author's note: A haircare professional can often provide insight on a variety of ways to deal with unsightly or unwanted hair, and can also offer advice tailored to your personal situation.)

A Few Tips Especially for the Ladies:

Although most of the strategies in this chapter apply to both men and women, here are some that apply mostly to the ladies.

23. Wear a Properly Fitting Bra.

A well-fitting bra can relieve back pain, lessen discomfort, allow for easier exercise routines, and save a person considerable embarrassment. Unfortunately, people can often tell if a woman is wearing an ill-fitting bra. Many specialty shops and department stores have individuals who can assist with measurement, style, and fit. Many are surprised at how much a person's appearance can change and how much better clothing hangs on the body when the undergarments are the right size and have the appropriate level of support. Because these items are worn all day and do so much work, it is important not to skimp on price–you usually get what you pay for.

24. Wear the Correct Shade of Lipstick.

It's sometimes difficult to tell if a person is wearing the correct color lipstick, but it's really easy to tell when an individual is not. It is important to spend some time checking out colors at a higher-end department store makeup counter and ask for opinions from the specialist. A good cosmetology professional will tell you the truth, regardless, and lead you to try and select colors that accentuate your complexion.

Similarly, makeup techniques and color usage can also date a person, as styles and products change over the decades. A department store cosmetologist can help show you techniques to minimize flaws without taking out a spatula and spackle. There are a variety of informative online videos to explore new ways to apply products, but the goal should always be to look ***healthy and natural***. A person should consider the face as a vintage canvas artwork–the point is to just touch-it-up to accentuate the beauty, not paint over it. Often, there is a fine line between glamor and garish, so when in doubt, *less is definitely more.*

(Author's Note: Use two mirrors and good lighting
to check for makeup lines. Select a foundation that

matches your skin tone and blend into the jaw, neck, and hairline to avoid unsightly blotches and marks.)

25. Keep Your Hairstyle and Makeup Current.

Be open to adjustments to your hairstyle and overall look. Sometimes even just a little twist–a difference in the part, a shorter cut, or change of color–gives a person a fresher, more up-to-date, and youthful look. This is where your trusted hairstylist comes into play. A hairstylist is always open to changes!

(Author's note: Don't mess with perfection! If you have a style and its "you," don't make any radical changes. Many hairstylists love to experiment with your hair, so sometimes it is best to make incremental changes toward a new style!)

26. Accessorize Tastefully.

Few things detract more from one's appearance than wearing too much jewelry. Few ladies need a ring on each finger, massive earrings, and five necklaces to be striking. Most times, gaudy jewelry and otherwise over-stated accessories only make an otherwise attractive woman look tacky. Always choose quality over quantity, as this projects class.

27. Throw Out the Seasonal Clothing Rules… Sometimes.

In these days and times, and especially depending on where a person lives, seasonal clothing rules may not be as important as they once were. It is OK to wear white pants in the fall, boots in the spring, and sandals in the winter (particularly if you live in Florida). These are perfectly acceptable fashion choices.

28. Confront Flabby Triceps.

These are "accessories" you didn't get overnight, so you won't lose them overnight either. The good news is there are exercises and diet adjustments that can lessen their impact on your appearance.

If you follow a good workout program that focuses on the triceps, including pushing exercises such as bench pressing, push-ups, and triceps extensions, the arms can be strengthened and tightened. Additionally, yoga, Pilates, and simple resistance training can be helpful as well.

29. Fight Facial Hair–and Win!

Some women struggle with unwanted facial hair, particularly after menopause. If this is a challenge, there are ways to remove it. One technique is to pluck it, and a good 10x lighted mirror is your best tool in this case. Some women employ threading or waxing for unsightly eyebrow, upper lip, or other problematic facial hair. These all work but they are temporary…and they hurt! Laser treatments are available and work on darker hair. This is generally effective for long-term hair removal after a few treatments. Probably the best option for most women is electrolysis. It is not only effective, but it is generally very reasonable in cost.

In Conclusion:

In this chapter, you have been exposed to many visible signs of physical aging and ways to deal with them. Some may directly affect you, but others may never be a factor. It is essential to be honest with yourself as to how these things affect you, your confidence, your interactions, and your ability to feel good about yourself. It is also comforting to know that for most issues, a person can take positive steps to minimize their impact.

Life is too short to waste time obsessing about minutiae, but it is also a happier life when we feel confident that we are presenting the best possible self we can at a given period in time. It is important to take steps as early as possible to prevent issues from becoming more complicated or difficult than they have to be.

With all that being said…

We are all our own worst critics, so we need to first love what is great about ourselves, address aspects that annoy us, and learn to live with flaws that are just a part of who we are. *True attractiveness and beauty come from the heart, the soul, and the sparkle in a person's eyes.* When a person knows and gladly accepts who he or she is with confidence, the person is well on the road to being a very attractive person–regardless of size, shape, age, fashion sense, or other attributes. Confidence and character are some of the best features a person can display.

CHAPTER NINE

STRATEGIES FOR FINDING PURPOSE

"Having a purpose and knowing exactly what your values are will add additional years to your life"

–Dan Buettner

Best-selling author, public speaker,

and holder of three Guinness World Records

Countless songs have been sung, books written, and speeches delivered over the millennia about the purpose of *purpose*. Many of the great thinkers, from ancient times to the present, have tried to explain what purpose is and why it is so important. They have used words like determination, focus, driving force, aim, goal, direction, passion, and intention when trying to explain it. All these terms are accurate to some degree, but in order to gain a firmer grasp of the importance of purpose, we need to delve into it a bit more deeply.

Purpose refers to the creation of meaning that gives us a sense of placement in our lives. When you have found purpose, it is easier to know where you belong.

Purpose is a fundamental part of living a fulfilling life. Many people wander through their existence with no direction and nothing to help them be productive and useful (or, at least, they feel that way). Losing purpose can happen at any juncture of life, and unfortunately, can happen many times as one progresses through careers, relationships, challenges, and other distractors.

Deep down inside, most of us know that we are meant for something greater than what we have, or who we are. We just don't know how to get the level of insight or knowledge that will unlock this potential and show us the way. Conversely, maybe we do know, but are not courageous or determined enough to follow the path to get there. People can fall into a trap of knowing what it would take to change or improve, but they become frightened or overwhelmed by the effort. As crazy as it may seem, many people fear success and the responsibilities that go with it. This hinders the realization of their full potential.

Some experts equate *purpose* with dreams. This makes sense, but first we must distinguish the difference between a *dream* and a *wish*. A *wish* is something we would like to have– a desire. A dream is something we would do anything to have or accomplish. A dream is something you feel you must have to be whole, and a wish (or desire) is something that would be nice to have, but it's OK if you don't. In that respect, *purpose* turns a desire into a goal, or dream, thus making it a very powerful force.

As you can see, a discussion about *purpose* is very complicated and confusing. It means many things to many people, so let's simplify it by saying that *purpose* is something you think about often; it makes you want to get out of bed in the morning. It is something that you really want to do– not just something you have to do. It is something that makes your creative juices flow. It is something that gives you direction in life.

Friedrich Nietzsche, a well-known, though often misunderstood, philosopher, got it right when he said, "He who has a 'why' to live for can bear almost any 'how.'" To his point, it's been noted that those in concentration camps during World War II who had a sense of *purpose* (e.g., family to find and reunite with, faith in God, and people to care for), had much better survival rates than those who did not. This same phenomenon is seen in wartime among soldiers, as well as among residents in assisted living facilities, nursing homes, and low-income housing developments. Those individuals who have a strong sense of *purpose* and an internal push to move forward, enjoy much better quality of life. They are able not only to perform essential duties and tasks appropriately but are also better able to help others around them.

The following pages include many strategies and suggestions that can be developed into a direction of purposefulness. They may be utilized temporarily or could be developed into an ongoing purpose that provides direction over a long period of time. It is vital for each person to find that spark that truly motivates action and sustains the type of personal growth that leads to happiness.

Many times, if a person goes forward with the idea of finding purpose, it won't happen. The best approach is to be constantly aware of those around you and to be open to situations where you can be useful. These events can be beneficial to you, your family, and your community, but they can also help you locate the inner calling of your purpose so you can develop into who you were meant to be. Many times, simple actions that appear to happen randomly can turn into long-lasting opportunities that develop into an undeniable reason and drive toward the fulfilling life we've been talking about.

1. Remove Yourself as the Center of Attention.

This is the first step to living a purposeful life. Although we need to accept that our lives are important, as we can't be helpful to others without taking care of ourselves, we need to make an effort to focus on the needs of others. It is not being suggested that we ignore our personal needs, but that we strive to find a balance between being the best person we can be, and equally helping others do the same.

2. Plan and Take A Trip.

Most of us love to take trips and one of the most satisfying parts of any travel is to make the plans yourself. It is invigorating to start the process of scheduling different aspects of a journey, regardless of mode of transportation and destination, and tying these items together for a successful and enjoyable time away. Besides the normal steps to planning a trip, consider these questions when planning:

1. Are there any travel restrictions that may come into play?

2. How involved with the "locals" in the area do you want to be?

3. How active do you want to be?

4. Should the time be strictly scheduled, or should it include some open time?

5. How much and how often will you need to communicate with those back home and the individuals where you are travelling?

6. What is the exchange rate for currency and is it readily available?

7. What happens if…? Have an idea for how to handle possible emergencies (e.g., illness, injury, missed flight, theft of items).

Planning a trip is a great way to rekindle enthusiasm for life and give you something to look forward to. Consider, also, planning with family or with friends. Time spent with loved ones and away from the grind of life and daily stressors can help a person regain the balance and insight to listen more closely to what makes them happy and satisfied. This whole process may spur you on to plan more trips and activities in the future.

(Author's note: For singles, travelling is a great way to more closely interact with others and develop relationships with similar-minded people.)

3. "Adopt" a Person.

There are so many opportunities and ways to share our lives with others who may be having challenges in theirs. Facilities such as nursing homes and assisted-living residences are always looking for (and readily welcome) visitors who have the time to spend with those who don't have friends and family to visit them on a regular basis.

If you're not sure how to make this happen, many religious organizations can match you up with individuals in the neediest situations. You just may be that angel someone is praying for. This can also be something that is done as a family, with children or teenagers who no longer have grandparents. Everyone has something that can be given as a gift to another person, such as the ability to sing, play an instrument, or just sit for an afternoon and play a card game.

(Author's note: My wife heard through our church that a nursing home was looking for people to visit residents. On her first day there, she introduced herself to a wheelchair-bound woman sitting off in

the corner by herself in the social room. For the next four years, she visited Wilma every week and they became very close, sharing a deep friendship until Wilma passed on. This time together was a blessing for both.)

4. Coach a Team.

Many of us have been involved in sports at some point in our lives and developed some skills and knowledge along the way. Why not put these to good use and coach a team? There are numerous opportunities to get involved. It can be done on a volunteer basis at many levels and could also become an income-producing situation if you are adept at teaching and relating information. It doesn't matter that you weren't a superstar when you played, as many truly great coaches were never outstanding players. They learned by listening and doing–the same skills you can pass on to others. Through coaching, you help players obtain the benefits of discipline and hard work, which builds their character and confidence. For many, there is no greater purpose in life.

If you are so inclined, contact your local school and sports organizations and put your "name in the hat." Even better, if you have a friend who is coaching, ask if he or she would like to have you around as an assistant.

5. Run for Office or Join a Local Board.

As discussed in Chapter Seven, running for office is a great way to impact the lives of others. Many public servants serve on school boards or act as members governing public agencies; these are volunteer positions that working and parenting adults often cannot spare the time to be involved in. Even the smallest positions provide many opportunities to make a positive change in an area, whether it be at the local, state, or national level. By starting small, you can learn the topography and then move to positions with increasing responsibility if you choose.

If you are a gifted communicator and have a willingness to serve, this is a great way to put purpose back into your life while helping others.

6. Write.

Everyone has an author inside who is calling out! There are so many writing opportunities available today. You could create articles for magazines, put together instruction manuals for products, write articles for newspapers (yes, they still exist!), create and maintain a website or blog, journal about transformative experiences, or even write that novel or children's book you've been putting together in your head for the last twenty years.

Writing is a great way to let those creative juices flow. It helps a person organize thoughts and develop ways to express them. It can help a person stay focused and mentally acute, provide an escape, or even act as a way to work through problems and concerns. There are many organizations that can help a person get started and provide outlets for written creations. Using your skills and engaging with others to develop further can provide a strong sense of purpose.

7. Incentivize and Reward Yourself for Important Accomplishments.

Sometimes we need a little kick in the butt to get something done. The easiest and most successful way of accomplishing a worthy goal is to tie a reward to its completion. Make the reward big enough to make you incentivized to do the work.

Rewarding yourself for a job well done is a great way to build some purpose into your life, complete short-term and long-term goals, and power through less-than-exciting tasks.

8. Take on A Part-Time Job.

If you are still in the work-a-day world, and have some spare time, consider picking up a part-time job to broaden your skillset, earn some extra spending money, or bridge to another career. There are many opportunities awaiting, and there are many companies and organizations that would love to have another dedicated employee on staff. Here are some considerations:

1. You could stay in your present field or choose a job that is outside of your realm of expertise so you can learn new skills. Either way, this is a good way to expand your horizons and keep broadening your abilities.

2. This is a great way to pay off any debt or build up an emergency or slush fund, as discussed in Chapter Six.

3. It is important to make sure you don't skimp on other important aspects of your life such as family time and worship.

4. Start the new job by writing down what you hope to obtain through the endeavor and keep a checklist of what you are getting out of the experience, allowing you to weigh costs and benefits. This will allow you to determine if it is worth continuing, if you should seek a new opportunity, or if you should place renewed effort elsewhere.

With that being said…

Even if you are not in the work-a-day world, a part-time job could give you a great reason to get out of the house and interact with others. It also provides a fuller schedule that can add purpose and enjoyment to each day, particularly if you are in a field that you love.

You could also choose to do something from home that could give you many great benefits as well, such as assisting with the care of grandchildren, working on a specific house project, or volunteering with a church group.

(Author's Note: A close friend, after his retirement, relocated across the country and was able to obtain a part-time position utilizing the same skills he used to become very successful financially.)

9. Organize and Run a Neighborhood Garage Sale.

This is a great opportunity to put your organizational skills into practice. There are so many things that have to be done to make a neighborhood sale successful. Scheduling, advertising, organizing, and assigning duties are just a few of the skills needed to pull this off.

This is a great time to use your gifts and skills to benefit your neighbors, and to even get to know them better.

10. Pursue a Hobby You Love.

Most successful people (at any stage of life) have a hobby they really enjoy that they spend quality time developing and sustaining. The benefits of having an activity that excites and interests cannot be overstated. A hobby keeps a person focused. It helps develop research skills and keeps a person current with technology and aspects outside the work-a-day world. It also helps a person meet new people with similar interests and gain new skillsets. It could possibly be used to earn a little extra money, and even help a person develop teaching or interpersonal skills that could be of use more broadly.

Here is a list of possible hobbies to give you an idea of the many choices available. In no way is it a complete list, but it may just lead to another idea that would excite you:

Learning a Musical Instrument	Officiating
Cooking	Pet Grooming
Coaching	Carpentry
Fitness Training	Furniture Construction
Reading	Boating
Crafting	Mapping
Computer Programming	Singing
Travel	Ancestry Research
Writing	Knitting/Crocheting
Political Action	Shopping
Painting	Electronics
Photography	Coloring
Bird Watching	Robotics
Poetry	Kayaking
Bible Study	Tai Chi or Yoga
Sewing	Volunteerism
Auto Repair	Collecting Items
Sports	Law/Legal Study
Pottery	Motivational Work
Hiking or Biking	Public Speaking
Home Improvement	Scouting
Coin Collecting	Wine Tasting
Making Jewelry	Paddleboarding

As you see, the list of hobby choices is essentially endless. The important thing is to find one that interests you and that you are passionate about. Also, there's no rule against having more than one!

11. Design That Invention That's Been in Your Head for So Long.

Stop dreaming about that useful gadget that's been on your mind forever and take positive steps to turn it into reality! Start with baby steps, like research and sketching, and then develop more detailed drawings. Find out what it takes to bring it to fruition and go for it! There are colleges and organizations where you can even have a prototype produced by 3D printing. Wouldn't it be horrible if someone else came up with the same idea and patented it before you could make up your mind to proceed?

12. Audit (or Enroll in) a College Class.

Most colleges and universities will allow you to take a class (physically or online) just for fun. It's called auditing a class. Auditing is free in some cases and at some institutions, or it may be offered at a reduced cost. Sometimes a person does not even have to be officially matriculated at the school.

Auditing a class is a great way to study a topic you've always been interested in, or even to become better acquainted with an area you wish to pursue as a hobby. It's also a great opportunity to increase your circle of friends in different age groups. And in the theme of "it's never too late," if you always wanted to take a few college classes or get a degree, that is also an excellent goal, no matter what your age or stage in life.

13. Become a "Gym Rat."

Joining a gym is one of the best ways to improve life–physically, mentally, and psychologically. A gym can also provide a great place to develop close friendships with like-minded people, broaden the age diversity in friendships, or just hang out and socialize. A couple things to take into consideration:

1. Don't forget the main reasons you joined the gym–keep your health goals at the forefront.

2. Take advantage of incentives. Many health insurance policies and employers will pay for a membership or offer discounted rates.

3. Learn by watching others.

4. Don't develop a reputation as a talker while using equipment.

5. Ask for advice. Most people love to give it.

6. Try to complete your workout before participating in the "gym social hour."

The gym is a great place to be for a lot of reasons. Who knows, you may be that reason that another person joins!

14. Join or Start a Book Club.

Book clubs are very popular, and for good reason. They provide an opportunity to be with people you know–or will get to know quickly. They give you a chance to be current in your reading exposure, learn and introspect, and express yourself in ways not usually available.

Book clubs are available in most communities, but it's often more fun to start one with like-minded friends.

15. Develop a New Software Program or App.

If you are computer savvy and have the inclination, there are ample opportunities to develop and maintain a software program or app. They can be developed for fun or can actually be useful. They could even become a money-making proposition.

Once you figure out which direction you want to go, research the steps needed and put your knowledge to good use.

16. Invest in Real Estate Fixer-Uppers.

Real estate investment can be a fascinating experience and very rewarding. It can also be a frustrating and expensive venture with many pitfalls along the way. If you are a process-oriented person, are handy with tools, and love the effort, it's worth your consideration.

Do your research for each project because every property is different. Don't be afraid to partner with others who have expertise in the building business or who have strengths that offset your weaknesses.

17. Go on a Mission Trip.

What better way to do good than to spend some time helping those who are less fortunate? Whether the destination is within US borders or in a less fortunate country, there are many options to choose from when looking to be of service to others.

Many churches and religious organizations have mission trips and opportunities for short- and long-term service, and it is a simple process to be a part of one of these efforts. There are opportunities that fit all abilities, from hurricane clean-up, to building a community well, ministering to the sick, or helping to teach children to read. Even mission trips that require physically demanding work still need a person to make meals and help with organization, so regardless of a person's physical stamina, there is almost always a role to be filled. You may have to jump through some hoops to qualify, but it is well worth the effort.

18. Become a Consultant.

This is a great way to extend your career and use the skills and knowledge you've accumulated over the years. The great thing about being a consultant is that you can usually work at your own pace and on your own schedule, but you don't have to actively chase new skills. It can also keep you in touch with many of those you previously worked with.

19. Volunteer.

Nothing screams *purpose* louder than acting as a volunteer. Whether you do it on a consistent basis or only occasionally, volunteering is one of the highest forms of service to others. There are so many options to reach out and be a blessing.

The following is a small list of possible opportunities for volunteering. There are so many other choices available, so it is important to be open to any options that may arise.

SPCA	Church Bus Driver
Service Clubs	Christmas Caroling
Classroom Helper	Rocking Premature Babies
Coaching	Pet Walking
Hospital Visitation	Trash Clean Up
Political Campaign Work	Refereeing
Scout Leader	Sports Concession Stand
Bell Ringer or Service Assistant	Walking the Elderly
	Sunday School Teacher
Meals on Wheels	Cooking or Shopping for Shut-Ins
Guardian Ad Litem	
Missionary Worker	Interpreter
Transportation for Those in Need	Homeless Shelter Work
	Arts and Crafts Classes
Crisis Hotline	Veterans' Associations
School Office Assistant	Habitat for Humanity
Babysitting	Grief Counselling
Visiting Nursing Homes	Homeowners' Association
Helping Elderly Neighbors	Neighborhood Watch
Mentoring Youth Groups	Financial Guidance
Suicide Hotline	Providing Music for Nursing Homes
Reading to the Blind	
Proofreader	Teaching Computer Literacy

Food Banks	Listener
Gathering for the Needy	Church Usher/Greeter
End-of-Life Counselling	Motivator/Coach
Pre-Cana Counselling	Airport Assistance
Travel Organization	Fitness Instructor

20. Keep a Daily "Self-Improvement To-Do List" and Update This List to Address New Goals.

This type of list is different from a daily schedule or calendar that you update on a day-to-day basis. It is designed to remind you to perform little tasks during the day that help you be a better person. They may consist of strategies, big or small, from many facets of life and can usually be done at any time throughout the day. You will find they do not consume much time at all, and the benefits, if done consistently, will be obvious.

This list is not designed to take the place of normal daily activities. It is meant to enhance these activities and enrich you as a person in terms of health, well-being, and personal growth. For example, below is my current list:

Ten-Item Daily Self-Improvement List:

Tai Chi 24 Form	Planks, Side, and Front
Drink at Least Six Glasses of Water	20-Minute Nap
	Daily Bible Reading
Tri-Stand	Face and Neck Massage
Table Back Stretch	Phone a Friend
Inversion Table	

What does this to-do list have to do with purpose? It keeps a person honest about his or her goals and reminds the individual of what has already been achieved. If you try incorporating this strategy for a month, you will see what I mean!

21. Tie Your *Purpose* to a *Higher Purpose*.

Whatever purpose you are pursuing, it should be somehow tied in with a *higher purpose*. Most people equate this higher purpose with God and a belief in a higher being. If this does not apply, perhaps internal motivation can be joined to the purpose of serving others above self, as this is also a noble goal.

Many, if not most, seek God's help and guidance in whatever they do and the decisions they make. Amazingly, when someone does this, it seems to give wings to that individual's purpose.

In Conclusion:

Living a *purposeful life* should be a constant pursuit, at any age. It is ultimately the responsibility of each individual to find and develop a purpose that drives and motivates both action and personal progression.

As discussed, there are many things that can be done to help a person achieve a purpose-filled life. Some of the ideas presented in this chapter may seem simple or inconsequential, but small changes can create ripples that lead to big differences overall. If these suggestions provide motivation and direction to better a person's life–or assist the individual in helping others–then that person is closer to achieving his or her overarching *life purpose*. There is a tremendous peace, contentment, and confidence that comes about when people feel meaning and value in their actions.

In the words of Pastor Rick Warren, author of *A Purpose Driven Life,*_"Purpose always produces passion." Living a fulfilling life requires each individual to find the passion that ignites life, giving the individual *purpose* to impact the world and others.

> *"Regardless of what I do, I know what my purpose is: to make a difference in people's lives"*
>
> –Tim Tebow,
> College All-American Football Player,
> Heisman Trophy Winner,
> NFL Quarterback, and Christian Missionary

CHAPTER TEN

PHYSICAL FITNESS STRATEGIES

*"If exercise could be packed into a pill,
it would be the single most widely prescribed and
beneficial medicine in the nation"*

—Robert Butler, MD
Director of the National Institute of Aging

The National Institute of Aging states that most people have never been told by a doctor to start an exercise program. This is mind-boggling, since doctors overwhelmingly believe that exercise is the solution for so many health problems. Doctors appear to be reluctant to talk to patients about fitness because they don't want to embarrass them or make them feel insecure.

Without passing judgment, let's entertain the following two facts: 1) exercise should be an extremely important component of each person's lifestyle, and 2) it is solely that individual's responsibility to make this happen. Let's face it: We all have reasons why we should spend time exercising. Unfortunately, many people believe it's too late in life to make any lasting improvements.

There are so many reasons (or should we say, *excuses*) why people do not include fitness in their daily routine: "I don't have enough time." "It's too expensive to belong to a club." "I don't have the right equipment." "I'm too old…" These are just some of the excuses used to avoid a structured fitness program.

There is so much evidence that points to the importance of being fit that it's hard to ignore how vital it is. The motivation is out there. And, if you don't find it, it most certainly will *find you* in the form of increased health issues. Pursuing and following a fitness-based lifestyle will have many positive effects, both physical and mental. When you are fit, you will feel better about yourself, look better, and you will have more stamina to do the things that you enjoy doing. Additionally, if you ever have any health problems or injuries, chances are you will have an easier time healing and overcoming these issues. For these reasons alone, it is important to become (and stay) fit.

In the following pages you will be exposed to many strategies that can put you on the path toward fitness or enhance what you are already doing. Many of these suggestions are simple to apply and easy to do. There are so many avenues to attaining higher fitness levels. One strategy is to set goals for the short-term that are achievable so that you can be bolstered by the results. Remember: Rome wasn't built in a day.

Also, keep this in mind: There is no quick fix when a person is out of shape. It may take time to see results and constant work to regain lost flexibility, strength, and balance. Some strategies will take a long time to actually attain success, and the measure of success may not be the same as we held at 25 years old. It is simply *consistent effort applied towards a goal* that moves a person in the right direction. And once you start, never stop–it's amazing how fast we lose the improvements we have worked so hard for if we aren't consistent with our efforts.

With that being said…

Living a fitness-based lifestyle is totally worth it! Read through this chapter a few times, set fitness goals with a trusted medical advisor, do your research, and get started. You will experience benefits you never thought possible!

1. Don't Expect to Pick Up Where You Left Off 20 Years Ago.

One of the biggest mistakes people make when they restart a fitness program is trying to pick up where they left off a long time ago. This is especially true for guys.

When you do decide to kickstart your training program after taking time off, ease back into the intensity aspect so that you don't injure yourself. This will also allow you to maintain the positive vibe that sustains your desire to get back in the saddle. There is nothing worse than trying to do good for your body–and then having your body kick you for it. To prevent injuries, it is best to dial up the weight, time, intensity, and repetitions gradually. Over time, and by preventing damage, you may be able to achieve some of the performance levels of the past.

Don't push it too hard, too soon!

2. Be Attuned to a Mind-Body Connection.

The connection between the mind and the body has been well documented over the years. What benefits the mind, benefits the body. And, what benefits the body, benefits the mind.

As you get more involved in fitness training, you will obviously notice improvement in your fitness levels, and you will also begin to see an uptick in mental acuity and mood. This can happen at any age and it doesn't take a rigorous fitness approach to achieve it.

3. Don't Expect Your Job to Keep You Fit.

People who have very physically demanding jobs often make the mistake of believing they don't need "extra" fitness activities. This is a huge mistake. Most jobs, no matter how physically challenging, do not give the all-encompassing fitness approach that can be found in a planned, scheduled training program. If you need to prove this to yourself, just try a Pilates routine–you'll find muscles you didn't know you had. Or engage in a cardio class–you will see that strength alone is not fitness.

If you have a physically demanding job, include it as a part of your training program but don't let it be a substitute.

4. Use It or Lose It.

Studies have shown how long it takes to lose fitness. The findings may surprise you. There are so many factors to consider, but there are some troubling findings that demand our attention:

1. The older a person is, the quicker he or she loses established fitness levels.

2. The *level of fitness* determines how fast a person loses it. It takes a highly fit person longer to lose the achieved benefits than an unfit person.

3. Different types of muscles lose their fitness levels more quickly than others.

4. A well-designed fitness program helps to keep a person on track to improvement.

5. Consistency breeds success. Inconsistency devolves into failure.

6. The biggest motivator is seeing or experiencing results.

The key? Once you get started, stay <u>consistent</u> with your training. If you slack off (for whatever reason), you will surely lose many of the benefits you worked so hard to accomplish.

5. Join a Gym with Full Awareness of the Pros and Cons.

Becoming a member of an established gym is a great way to ramp up fitness training; however, there are pros and cons to joining a gym.

PROS:

1. You have trainers at your disposal who can help guide you in the use of techniques that support your fitness goals.

2. You have access to many fitness-testing and evaluation tools.

3. You will be spending time with like-minded people who probably share many of your same goals.

4. You will have access to much more (and much better) equipment.

5. There are usually several local options. Many gyms offer facilities at multiple locations so you can get your workout in while travelling.

6. You can take advantage of a free-trial membership to ensure the gym is a good fit.

7. Many gyms offer a discount for multi-person or family memberships.

8. You can benefit and learn by observing others.

9. Many gyms have features such as classes, saunas, showers, or pools that can be utilized at no extra charge.

10. Just making the effort to be there is a big motivator and puts your mindset in the right place.

11. The social aspect of a gym cannot be overstated.

12. Many insurance programs and employers offer a gym membership (or a discount) as a benefit.

13. The gym is a great place to network more broadly.

Cons

1. Gym memberships can be costly. Many gyms expect a person to join for at least a year, or have a required, upfront registration fee.

2. Popular gyms may be crowded at different times during the day.

3. Many gyms, if not most, have gawkers and those who want to talk, not train.

4. It can be hard to concentrate on a workout because of a multitude of distractions.

5. Gyms aren't always open when a person wants or needs to train due to personal and professional time constraints.

6. Gyms have dress codes for proper attire, including a shirt and shoes.

7. Many gyms may not be up to your personal cleanliness
    standards.

It's been said that approximately 50 percent of the people who join a gym never see the inside of it again after a few workouts. Whether or not you join a gym for fitness training is a personal decision, so if you find one that interests you, take advantage of any trial membership period offered. You should be able to decide if the location and services are a good fit during this period.

> *(Author's note: My wife and I belong to a gym, but we also have a home gym. Over the years, we have equipped it with much of the same equipment available at a commercial gym. We use both gyms often, but for different reasons and benefits!)*

6. Warm Up Before You Start–Physically AND Mentally.

If you want to make your training sessions more beneficial, warm up. It's vital to get your body and mind prepared so you don't feel like you are just going through the motions.

Here are some suggestions to help you prepare for a great workout:

1. Spend a few minutes reviewing your busy day and put
    it on hold during your workout time.

2. Before your workout, deal with any situations that may interrupt your workout time, and put your phone away (e.g., avoid emails and calls).

3. Make sure you have all the essential clothing and equipment before you start.

4. Spend a few minutes planning the workout in detail before beginning. Know what you are going to do before you start.

5. Always start the routine with less intensity and work up to (or near to) maximum levels, depending on what you're trying to accomplish.

6. Allow your body to be your guide–sometimes it is not a good day to try to achieve a higher level.

7. Consider any problem areas that need more focus and work them into a training regimen.

8. 8. Consider any injuries you may need to work around and design low or no-impact activities to assist with healing (e.g., walking or water-based exercise).

7. Don't Compare Yourself to Others.

Never compare yourself and your training to anyone else. Each person is different, and each person's goals are different. Two things can happen when a person plays the comparison game: 1) you can become frustrated if you are not keeping up, or 2) you can develop a false sense of achievement if you are more advanced than others.

The best way to keep yourself from comparing is to have a firm grasp of your goals and a firm understanding of your action plan. Keeping track of fitness goals on a chart and recording daily work-out routines keeps the focus on you and your personal achievements. A good way to do this is to keep a chart or journal that lists the weight values, repetitions, sets, activity times, and other information about routines. This helps to motivate a person by providing tangible evidence of increased fitness and personal development.

8. Train Before You Go Home from Work or Other Duties.

If the only time you can train at the gym is after a long day, plan to get it done **before** you go home. If you make a stop at the house before completing a workout, chances are you will get distracted and find excuses not to go.

Plan to wind down from your day after your workout!

9. Consider Muscle Strength and Muscle Endurance.

Simply stated, muscle strength is measured through muscle exertion for a brief period of time, while muscle endurance is measured through muscle exertion over an extended period of time. According to Bodybuilding.com (2017), the National

Football League uses a basic test for each: For muscle strength, it's how much weight a player can bench press once; for muscle endurance, it's how many times a player can bench press 225 pounds in one set.

Which is more important? Each of these play a major role in fitness at any age and can affect activity, endurance, and mobility levels.

To train muscular strength, an accepted rule in weight training is to do sets of four to ten repetitions with a weight close to the person's maximum capability, usually with a longer rest period between sets. To train muscle endurance, the person can complete sets of 15 to 20 repetitions with less weight and reduce the time between sets. Muscle endurance can (and should) also be trained by incorporating cardiovascular activities such as running, walking, swimming, or biking.

A weakness in either muscle strength or muscle endurance can have adverse effects at any point in life and can especially affect individuals as they get older. A good, consistent fitness program containing both types of training helps alleviate many problems that could arise from either.

10. Don't Just Lose Weight – Lose Fat and Build Muscle.

Too many people are driven by their weight. People often say their weight is fine because they weigh the same amount as they did in high school. This is not an accurate way to evaluate fitness.

When a person is younger, weight is generally composed of more muscle, proportionally speaking. As a person ages, there is a strong tendency, though not intentionally, to lose muscle mass and replace it with fat mass. This does not have to happen.

Approaching weight in a different way can be helpful. Get in a mindset of training for losing fat and do not be concerned about your weight as a number. If you are training properly, you likely won't lose as much weight because you will be adding muscle weight as you train. Muscle weighs more than fat, but it has a lot more benefits to the overall health of the person.

It is a good idea to meet with a trusted certified trainer; he or she can design a program specifically for your needs and goals.

11. Train with a Partner.

A good workout partner serves many purposes. This person can help develop the program, provide encouragement during workouts, and be the motivation to show up for training sessions. When determining a workout partner:

1. Be selective. Don't choose one just to have one. At some point you will know who this person should be.

2. Make sure your schedules coordinate on a consistent basis.

3. Know each other's goals, strengths, and weaknesses.

4. Research together.

5. Commit to the partnership and work to motivate each other.

A good workout partner is invaluable to helping achieve fitness goals. Find the right one and become a great partner yourself. You will be able to accomplish much more than you would if you were training alone.

12. Consider Cardiovascular AND Resistance Training.

Years ago, the prevailing belief was that cardiovascular training was superior to resistance training as a fitness activity. We now understand that both are equally important.

There is good news. You can work on and improve both aspects of fitness at the same time. Any activity that raises your heart rate and keeps it up for a period of time can benefit cardiovascular training goals. That can be achieved by walking, running, cycling, and swimming, but also by lifting weights as well. It is important to learn how to calculate your target heart rate (THR) and use this as a guide while working out. The formula requires subtracting the age of the person from 220 (this provides the maximum heart rate); this value is then multiplied by both 0.60 and 0.80 to obtain a range for the THR.

Resistance training requires the use of weights (e.g., free weights, machines, body weight) to put stress on muscle groups, causing them to get stronger. Many cardio programs incorporate resistance training. There is a lot of information available on both of these types of training, so don't hesitate to utilize a trusted personal trainer's knowledge and expertise to help plan a program best suited to your individual needs.

13. Explore HIIT Workouts.

HIIT stands for High-Intensity Interval Training. It involves maximum effort for a short period of time alternated with a period of less effort. It can be done for both cardio and weight-training activities. These activities can also be combined.

There are many upsides of HIIT. It allows you to complete a workout in a shorter period of time. It increases your metabolism, which helps a person to use and burn energy, and it increases post-exercise fat burning capabilities.

There are some downsides to HIIT. It increases the risk of injury because of the intensity, and it can cause longer periods of fatigue. It can also cause mental burn out.

So how much should you do? The general rule of thumb says that two days a week is sufficient if you build in at least a full 48-hour rest period between sessions.

> *(Author's Note: HIIT is not for everyone, and it is certainly not the place to start in a workout routine, but if you decide to add this to an already intense training repertoire, start off slowly by working this into two workouts a week and monitor for any possible injuries or unusual fatigue).*

14. Confuse Your Muscles.

One of the most effective concepts of weight training is called the "muscle confusion" concept. The idea is to vary workouts so that muscles do not adapt to the same exercises, causing them not to respond as effectively as they should.

The best way to approach this is to change workouts often. This serves two purposes. It keeps your training from hitting a plateau, and it helps to keep you interested in your fitness program.

15. Consult with a Trusted Medical Advisor about Taking Creatine.

Creatine is probably the number one supplement used for improving performance in the gym and in athletics. Studies indicate it may increase strength, muscle mass, athletic performance, and recovery after training.

Just what is creatine? Without getting complicated, it is a substance found naturally in muscle cells that helps produce and store energy during workouts and high-intensity activities. It has also been credited with benefiting brain function in older people.

There are some concerns about the long-term safety of creatine. Some studies indicate that creatine may cause digestive and cardiovascular problems, and possibly raise the risk of cancer, although this information is still considered inconclusive.

If you are considering the use of creatine, it is important to consult with your trusted medical advisor to make sure you are drinking enough water and are a good candidate for this supplement. There have been cases of dehydration and other severe health complications in athletes taking creatine. As with any product or supplement, it is important for a medical professional to evaluate any possible interactions with medications or health conditions prior to usage.

16. Eat Enough Protein.

Protein is a nutrient essential for building and repairing muscle mass. It is an important component of every cell in the body.

It is vital to consume enough protein on a daily basis, but different people have different needs. Generally speaking, a sedentary male needs approximately 60 to 70 grams of protein a day, while a sedentary female needs approximately 40 to 50 grams per day. This whole equation changes when one is involved in a rigorous training program. An actively training person requires approximately 1-1.5 grams of protein per day per kilogram of bodyweight (i.e., divide weight in pounds by 2.2 to find the weight in kilograms).

A person should consider these factors when adjusting protein intake:

1. Animal protein from meat is considered a "complete protein source," while many plant-based sources of protein lack some of the essential amino acids.

2. It is important to limit the intake of processed meats.

3. Lean sources of protein are best.

4. It is a good idea to spread protein consumption throughout the day.

5. Protein supplements are readily available and are very reasonably priced.

6. Vegans should take a protein supplement to offset the lack of complete protein in plant-based sources. *(Author's note: Quinoa and soy are considered complete plant-based sources.)*

7. Consume approximately one-third of daily protein within an hour of the completion of a strenuous muscle-building training session.

8. When first adding more protein to the diet, increase the amount over a period of time so the body can adjust to the higher amino acid load.

9. Discuss any dietary adjustments with a trusted medical advisor prior to undertaking a new regimen, especially if you have, or suspect that you have, kidney dysfunction.

Consistent protein intake can bolster training efforts and provide better results.

17. Rest Your Muscles.

A good workout breaks down muscle tissue. Rest allows tissue to rebuild. It is imperative to give muscles a chance to recuperate after being pushed to (or near) exhaustion.

Here are some guidelines:

1. Large muscle groups should be rested for at least 48 hours between intense workouts.

2. Small muscle groups should be rested at least 24 hours between intense workouts.

3. Muscle groups should not be trained intensely more than twice a week.

4. It is important to rarely, if ever, work out the same muscle group two days in a row.

5. Muscles should be "fed" with protein during the recuperation period.

6. A good massage can help in recuperation.

Many guys, especially those just starting out and wanting to make great gains quickly, train the same muscle groups every day. This is not a good idea as it increases the chance of injury. It is important to give areas a chance to recuperate.

18. Understand Functional Fitness.

Functional fitness is training that prepares you for everyday tasks and movements. It mimics movements performed on a daily basis that usually involve many muscle groups and joints. These could include squats, lunges, cardio movements, and exercises that require the body to change directions and levels.

What good is a muscular, "pretty body" that struggles to perform even the basic actions that are part of day-to-day existence? A flattering backside is desirable, but if a person can't even bend over to pick something up off the floor without losing balance, the pomp has no circumstance.

Functional fitness training can be done with or without props or equipment. Many functional training programs include the use of free weights, medicine balls, ropes and other props that allow free movement while engaging multiple muscle groups and joints. There are others that can be done at home with little or no equipment.

Most gyms offer classes in functional fitness and have trainers that are adept at sculpting a program to fit most personal needs.

(Author's Note: Many functional fitness activities were previously mentioned in Chapter 4 under the strategies for use while watching television.)

19. Hydrate During Training.

Water is the essence of life and most people do not drink enough. Consuming water during training sessions is important because it helps cells recuperate while they are working and keeps a person from dehydrating. The body must have more water during times of exertion.

Gyms have plenty of water fountains, or a person can bring a personal bottle. Many running paths and trails have water available during most hours of the day. If you start losing energy or feel light-headed during training, chances are that you are dehydrated.

20. Start Recovery Right After Training.

Recovery after an intense workout should begin immediately. As soon as you can after finishing, take a hot shower. This will help to alleviate some (if not all) of the pain or soreness you may be having from your workout. Follow this with a cold shower to help reenergize.

After a shower, drink a glass of water and follow it with about 8-12 ounces of chocolate milk. A study reported in WebMD (2010) showed that fat-free chocolate milk is a great option to refresh and replenish protein supplies that are exhausted during a workout. In the hour following, the person can make a protein shake with protein powder or have a regular meal that is high in protein (Laino, 2010).

Following this routine will help a person recover much quicker and be ready for the next session.

21. Don't Forget Your Legs!

Have you ever seen a guy at the beach with a sculpted upper body who has scrawny legs? Many men focus so heavily on upper body strength that they neglect working on their legs. As difficult as legs are to train, it is never a good idea to go light on them. Legs require a major expenditure of energy to work out, but they usually respond well.

Luckily, there are many ways to train legs without even stepping into a gym. One simple but effective exercise is the Tri-Stand. It's designed to work the legs but is also great for the core and the gluteal muscles (i.e., the backside). To complete a Tri-Stand, a person should stand straight, suck in the abdominal muscles, tense the gluteal muscles, bend at the knees, and hold the position, working up to about 20 minutes. This won't build large muscle size in the legs, but it will make them stronger and more functional.

Additional to this, it is important not to rely on running or walking to develop leg strength. You won't get the size results, which will be disappointing. In order to increase the build of leg muscles, a person must work them out with heavy resistance training no more than twice a week.

22. Measure Progress, but Don't Obsess.

There are so many devices available today designed to monitor and chart workouts. Warning: Don't fall into the trap of spending so much time compiling and recording results that you skimp on your training. If you find yourself overdoing the monitoring and documentation, get refocused on actual training methods and the rest should take care of itself.

23. Understand the Difference Between Soreness and Pain.

After a workout, soreness is a healthy and expected result; however, pain may be an indication of injury. The problem is, pain is not always consistent, and the seriousness of an injury does not always equal the level of pain.

How do you tell the difference? **Time** helps differentiate between the two. Soreness usually lasts about two to three days (depending on the intensity of the workout), but pain usually lingers for a longer period of time, and it will probably restrict movement, limiting the ability to train effectively. Pain is often "sharper" and "louder" in its intensity.

You know your body better than anyone, and it's important to understand that each person's body reacts differently to the stresses of physical activity. If the sensation persists over a week or so, it is important to have it checked so you do not injure yourself further.

With all that being said…

While it is not always easy to differentiate between pain and soreness, you can treat both by applying heat or ice.

Ice should be applied to muscle strains and joint sprains; swollen, red, or hot body parts; and areas of acute pain. Heat should be applied to muscle pain or soreness, stiff joints, arthritis, and recurrent injuries. Heat or ice can be applied for 20 minutes, followed by 20 minutes "off." This should be done repeatedly over a period of a couple hours. Heat and ice can both help in alleviating pain. After a couple days, it is important to reevaluate the discomfort to decide if it's soreness or pain.

Too many people overlook obvious pain caused by injury for a number of reasons. ***If you suspect you have an injury that could affect your training or cause further problems, it is important to stop training immediately and have it checked out by a trusted medical advisor.***

> *(Author's Note: NSAIDS (nonsteroidal anti-inflammatory drugs) are also good at decreasing the localized inflammation that causes pain, but these can also cause gastrointestinal irritation and canker sores, among other more serious problems, in some people.)*

24. Use a Compression Belt.

Do yourself a favor and spend $15 to $20 on an elastic, Velcro-fastening compression belt. It can serve many purposes. It can be worn during workouts for back support or to help in correcting posture during activities. What they are really designed for is to trim the waist. Obviously, these won't burn fat, but they will help you to contract your core muscles, which will make you look and feel slimmer. Is it a temporary fix? Probably, but it can be an added reminder to suck that gut in!

25. Cross-Train.

Cross-training refers to utilizing activities within a training regimen that are not usually associated with the main fitness focus. Many athletes use cross-training because it benefits them in ways a regular sport can't. A good example would be the football player who plays racquetball in the off-season to develop his coordination and footwork.

How do you include cross-training in workouts? It's pretty simple, actually. For strength training, a person can use different kinds of weights such as free weights, machines, and body-weight exercises for the same muscle group. For endurance training a person can run, do intervals, bike, swim, or play soccer.

One of the greatest benefits of cross-training is that it keeps a person from getting bored with a fitness program. It also tends to help a person work muscles that are not emphasized in the usual routine. Many people have the same basic workout schedule and program but adjust it by utilizing different equipment and techniques each time they train.

26. Park and Walk.

Instead of parking right in front of the store, park at the other end of the lot and walk. In fact, hoof it. This is a great way to force yourself to do a mini cardio workout!

27. Don't Weigh Yourself Every Day.

If weight is a concern, regardless of whether you are trying to gain or lose–do not monitor the scale on a day-to-day basis. This is not a good indication of progress because weight fluctuates naturally, depending on activity level, food consumption, and liquid intake.

If, for some reason, you still feel compelled to constantly check your weight, make sure you do it at the same time each day, under the same circumstances, and on the same scale.

28. Use the Two-Muscle-Group Training Method.

One of the most popular weight training programs is the two-muscle-group method. This consists of focusing on two groups of muscles at each work out and doing exercises that are specifically designed for these groups. The most accepted approach is to group chest muscles and triceps on the first day, the back and biceps the next day, quads and hamstrings the third day, and shoulders and abdominals on the fourth.

The grouping can be changed every few weeks and, using cross-training, a person can alter the exercises to keep it fresh.

With all that being said…

There are many other approaches that can be used effectively with weight training programs. Some use a complete body workout, others do upper body one day and lower body the next. Still others will work the pulling muscles one day and the pushing muscles the next. It is essential to make sure you spend time doing resistance exercises and get smart about adding in activities. A good program includes working smart AND working hard.

The bottom line: Train on a consistent basis and learn what works best for you.

29. Avoid Testosterone Boosters.

We are inundated with advertisements touting the benefits of testosterone boosters. The advertised benefits are overblown, exaggerated, and largely untested. They can also be unsafe, affecting delicately balanced natural hormone levels. Excess testosterone can be converted into estrogen or cholesterol.

Before considering testosterone (or any other supplement) it is important to check with a trusted medical advisor regarding the safety and benefit of the substance.

30. Ride A Bike.

Bicycling is an excellent way to train cardio. It's fun, energizing, and can be very social. Biking is also a great way to cross-train. You can rotate it with other cardio exercises by riding on different terrain or by doing intervals on flat surfaces and steep hills.

Most bike shops will let you test out a bike prior to making a purchase. Take advantage of this opportunity and find one that you will really enjoy riding. It's better to spend a little extra on one that you will truly use.

> *(Author's note: Don't forget to wear a helmet. You may even want to wear cycling gloves if you are riding over rough terrain.)*

31. Train in the Pool.

The swimming pool is a fantastic place to train. There are so many activities that can be done in the water, both for cardio and resistance training. The only restrictions are your imagination and the number of people in the pool at the time. Additionally, pool-based training is a great way bridge to higher levels of activity for individuals who have balance issues, are healing from prior injuries, or are in poorer or frailer condition, as falling is less of a concern and the body weight is supported in water.

Here is a small list of possible training options:

Swimming "Lazy" Laps	Swimming Sprints
Boxing	Sprinting Laps
Marching	Breathing Control
Rope Climbing	Resistance with Weights
Water Karate	Wrestling
Partner Carrying	Treading Water
Walking Laps	Sports-Related Movements

If you are fortunate enough to have access to a swimming pool, use it to your advantage for training and enjoy yet another type of cross-training.

(Author's note: The pool is a great place to do rehabilitation training while recovering from injury. Just always remember to follow the advice of your trusted medical advisor in beginning and increasing any training.)

32. Train Even While You Are Away from Home.

Being away from home is no excuse to skip a workout. Many gyms have multiple locations; others offer a single-day pass. Many hotels have gym or pool facilities on premises. If none of those options are available, you can always find a location such as a school that has a track for running and walking.

33. Remember: Your Best Training Days are When You Don't Want to Train.

We all have days where we just don't feel like training. That's very natural. Life gets in the way.

Interestingly, many times it is the days where we don't even want to think about working out that we have our best workouts! Remember this when you feel too tired to get it done!

34. Listen to and Follow the Experts.

Regardless of your fitness level and goals for change, the following websites are great sources for information for how to plan, set-up and implement your training program:

1. www.verywellfit.com,

2. www.muscleandfitness.com,

3. www.bodybuilding.com and

4. www.nerdfitness.com

In Conclusion:

There is no proof that fitness will guarantee a longer life (although there is a lot of supporting evidence).

There *is* conclusive evidence, however, that living a fitness-based lifestyle does, generally, allow for ***better quality of life***.

Fitness involves an effective ongoing exercise program, and this affects our lives positively in so many different ways. It helps us to look and feel better, reduce stress, recover from injury or sickness faster, lose weight, and gain muscle. It helps us to perform everyday tasks with much less effort and enhances our mental capabilities. It may even extend the time of independence and functionality that we can expect from our bodies. There are so many reasons to follow a good exercise program that we are really selling ourselves short if we don't.

The great thing is that it is never too late to embark on a solid and effective fitness program. Obviously, it is better to start when we're younger, but even at an advanced age, the benefits to health and well-being are undeniable.

"Physical fitness is not only one of the most important keys to a healthy body, it is the basis of dynamic and creative intellectual activity."

–JFK
One of the Coolest Presidents Ever

CHAPTER ELEVEN

MINDFULNESS STRATEGIES

"Be mindful in the moment, that's enough.
Each moment is all we need, not more."

–Mother Teresa
Missionary, Nun
Nobel Peace Prize Winner,
Saint

An article in *Psychology Today* refers to mindfulness as a "state of active, open intentional attention on the present," 'without judgment of one's thoughts and feelings.' It involves "letting go and being yourself in the moment," and being present 'in the here and now without being distracted by the past or future' (Dixit, 2008).

Mindfulness has its roots in ancient religions practiced thousands of years ago. Recently it has gained popularity in the West, and it can be melded synergistically into many Judeo-Christian beliefs and practices.

Many clinical practitioners have come to realize that mindfulness is a great process for dealing with stress, depression, and anxiety. It can also help people better cope with isolation and rejection.

Some people love to rehash the past. For whatever reason, they feel comfortable there, even if it wasn't a pleasant time for them. Many would rather deal with aspects of their lives they recognize and are familiar with. Others fear the future, mostly because they don't have a clue about what lies ahead. Mindfulness is a great tool to help alleviate these patterns of thinking.

There are many ways to practice mindfulness and they depend on focusing on the _now_. This chapter presents some strategies to develop a "mindfulness mentality" by learning some tried and true techniques. Some will be simple to follow, while others will need practice to make them effective.

Since mindfulness can (and should) become a way of life, you will also learn some everyday strategies that help to make life more peaceful and focused.

1. Accept that Everything Happens for a Reason.

Every action that happens in the universe, no matter how seemingly unimportant, happens for a reason. You may never know why you took that wrong turn, dropped that glass on the floor, or ran into that long-lost friend, but it led to further events that are part of a larger plan. It is important to just accept the fact that what happens–the good and the bad–all has some impact on your life, or someone else's. Each event is intertwined and layered with others to produce the *now*.

In this respect, it is less important to attempt to understand why things occur–but rather to accept that what *is*, is what *is supposed to be*. Many times, the reason for events will be revealed to you at some point.

2. Clean Off Your "Desk."

When settling in to work on a job or project, get rid of all the distractions that can keep you from the task at hand. Remove all the notes, tools, clutter, and anything else that could slow down or distract your progress. This would include any electronic devices not directly associated with or needed to complete what's in front of you.

3. Multi-Task Sparingly.

Multi-tasking is a way of life for many. We feel we are getting more done by bouncing from task to task. Sometimes that's true, but it comes with a price. If we are not able to give something our full attention, chances are we will have to come back later to make it right.

There are obviously situations that will require moving from one task to another in the same time frame, so try to organize your time and don't let multi-tasking dominate your life.

4. Live in the Moment, Even if It's Not Enjoyable.

Every moment we have is a blessing, so we need to be *present* to live these moments to their fullest–even when they are unpleasant. Remember that everything happens for a reason–even if the reason is to teach us something or to redirect our priorities. These not-so-enjoyable moments have been given to us to affect our lives in some way, so it is important to be fully engaged.

5. Focus on Those You Are With.

When in the presence of another person, focus your total attention on him or her. As mentioned in Chapter Five, treat this person like he or she is the most important person in your life at that moment. Put aside all distractions that could even remotely make the person think you are not paying attention. Let the individual know that he or she is important, and that you value the time spent together.

6. Start the Day Without Electronic Devices.

Get out of the habit of starting the day by first picking up and using a phone or computer when you get up in the morning. By leaving these items tucked away for a while, it allows you to ease into the day and not get bombarded by the news or your daily workload. It also gives you a better opportunity to interact with those closest to you without distraction and to mentally focus on the more important things in life.

It may take a while to get out of the habit, but if you are able to start your mornings without your phone or computer, you will probably find yourself more focused and productive during the rest of the day.

(Author's Note: In general, compartmentalizing cell phone and computer usage into certain periods of the day can allow you to better engage with the people and events that make life worth living. It also saves time that is wasted, making a person more productive.)

7. Connect with Nature.

The world around us has so much to offer, but we rarely see the most beautiful parts of it. Spending time observing and interacting with nature is one of the most relaxing and mindful exercises. Depending on where a person lives, there are many opportunities to experience what nature shares with us. Even if you live in a large metropolitan area, there are ample opportunities to take in nature and its beauty.

Here are some suggestions for connecting more closely with the natural world:

1. Add nature-friendly plants to your landscaping.

2. Put up a bird feeder…or two or three.

3. Visit some of the many nature trails and parks in your area.

4. Go camping.

5. Rise early in the morning and experience a sunrise and the increased animal activity.

6. Obtain a telescope and observe the heavens.

7. Drink a morning beverage on the patio or while peering out a window.

8. If you live in town or within a city, leave for a while.

9. Go fishing–and hope the fish don't bother you!

10. Ride a horse

11. Look for opportunities to get off the beaten path by travelling to state and national parks.

The opportunities to engulf yourself in the natural world are endless. You just have to be willing to seek them out and take advantage of them.

8. Devote Yourself Entirely When Making Important Commitments.

We make many commitments in life. Some are important. Some are not. Some are short. Some are of longer duration. It is important not to leave unfinished plans due to half-hearted attempts, or to start something without realizing how much dedication and effort it involves. Do your homework before making the mistake of committing to something that you won't be able to devote sufficient time and energy toward completing or doing right.

9. Practice Staying in the *Now.*

Regardless of what you are doing, practice living life moment by moment. Although this can be difficult, with a little practice, it is possible to master the art of concentration, allowing you to be present and a part of each moment you experience. It is well worth the effort!

10. Take One Day at a Time.

Taking one day at a time is the essence of mindfulness. If you can focus on today and not deal with tomorrow and all its duties and worries, you are way ahead of the game.

One of the best tools to help accomplish this is a daily planner. If you know what's expected of tomorrow, you probably don't have to worry about it (well, at least not as much as if you had no idea what was going to happen and what you might have forgotten…).

The best time to fill out an agenda (daily planner) is at night while you review the day you just lived. This is a great way to better control your life, set goals, and celebrate accomplishments (as we are actively taking the time to notice that they have occurred). It also makes the activities and duties more manageable, as there are less distractions.

11. Know Your Long-Range Goals and Plans.

If you have taken the time and made the effort to prepare for the future, you will know where you are headed and what needs to be done to get there. This act of planning makes it much easier to take life one day at a time because it removes the necessity of constantly worrying about what lies ahead of you.

With that being said…

Life can be great one month and terrible the next. It takes some crazy twists and turns. Sometimes we are on top of the world and other times we feel the world is crashing down on us. Taking control of our future and living in the present makes these life fluctuations much easier to accept and manage, and allows for more balance in perspective.

12. Relegate Your Regrets to the Back Burner.

We all have done crazy things in our past. Some we wish we had never done. Some we wish we could redo, and perhaps we feel we would if we had the chance. But we can't go back and alter what we've already done. Sure, we can try to make it right and apologize, but many times these efforts are futile.

The best approach is to face past regrets, deal with the fallout–whatever it takes–and then put these issues aside. Make sure they stay in the past and don't keep popping up to haunt your present and future life. It is valuable to remember that this is a good practice for how you interact with others as well. Once a mistake is atoned for, it needs to be relegated to *both of your pasts.* If this is not possible, the relationship may be unlikely to continue–or at least, it is unlikely to grow and flourish.

As always, there is no shame in seeking professional help to manage regrets or pain that interferes with the ability to truly enjoy life. It is better to solicit advice from a trusted mental health advisor and find a way to mitigate these feelings than to lose precious years of happiness to what ultimately cannot be erased.

13. Learn to Refocus from Distractions.

Distractions are a part of life–learn to deal with them. If they are important, focus your attention and make sure they are just temporary. If they are not important, dismiss them and refocus your attention to the task at hand. Use one of the structured exercises in Strategy 19 of this chapter to help you refocus. Deep breathing and mindful gazing are very effective techniques.

14. Utilize Delayed Gratification.

A great way to stay in the *now* is to practice delayed gratification. Simply stated, if you want something, set it aside as a reward for achieving a goal.

Here's a great example. Say you want a new car and know exactly the model you want–and you can afford it. Instead of just going out to buy it, set a goal to get your mile run time down to a certain number of minutes. When you achieve your goal, you get the car–simple as that!

This reward system, as previously discussed in Chapter Nine, is a great way to focus on a segment of life that may be important but requires a little nudge to retain your attention.

15. Be Curious but Don't "Seek" in Unproductive Ways.

Curiosity can be a blessing. It helps us discover new ideas, meet new people, and experience new journeys. It can even motivate us to step away from our normal lives and expand our horizons.

We need to, however, be careful not to get bogged down on the minutiae created by curiosity, as it can be very distracting. It is a dangerous cycle to constantly play what-if games or question why events occurred. It is far better to harness this energy for more productive aspects of life. Better to slow down, relax, and refocus so we can stay in the *now*.

This is also true in relationships. If a person shares private information, this is often a testament to your bond. But, within confidential discussions, do not seek details that are not your business or are unnecessary to providing assistance. Sometimes being mindful in a friendship means being a devout, and nearly silent, listener.

16. Embrace the Stillness.

We live in a fast-paced world that is ever changing, seemingly at warp speed. We have many day-to-day, minute-to-minute distractions that keep us from relaxing.

At some point in each day, find a quiet, still, free-from-distraction location and spend some time there. It doesn't have to be long; maybe just 15 to 20 minutes. You don't have to sleep. Do some deep breathing to help take your mind off the world. Above all–relax.

You may find it difficult to do this at first, but with a little practice, you will be able to come back to the world more alert and better equipped to complete your day with the results you desire.

17. Unleash the Power of Prayer.

Prayer is a powerful form of mindfulness. Simply put, it is communication with God. But prayer is also so much more. It is a mindful activity that allows us to free ourselves from distractions and focus intently on the *now*. It also helps us form a deeper, more intimate connection with God.

Prayer can be verbal or silent, and comes in many forms: formal, informal, written, and spoken; prayer can even be done through song. There are prayers asking for for-giveness, prayers requesting favors, and prayers expressing thankfulness.

Prayer is a driving force in every religion, but it also plays a role in the lives of many others who do not profess any form of religion.

With that being said…

18. Use Quiet Time to Let God Speak to You.

So many times, we try to tell God how things ought to be or how we want them to be. Consider instead doing this: After you finish telling Him what you think, sit back, relax and let Him tell you what HE thinks. It is amazing what we can "hear" when we give God a chance to let us know His plans for us.

19. Try These Structured Exercises to Develop and Practice Mindfulness.

Although there are many structured exercises to help a person to develop and practice mindfulness, the following are a few that are widely accepted as being effective and simple to perform.

1. Sitting Meditation: Sit comfortably with your back straight and hands relaxed in your lap or on your thighs. Close your eyes. Breathe deeply–in through your nose and out through your mouth. Focus on each

breath. Continue doing this for a few minutes and work up to 20 minutes. When your thoughts wander, acknowledge their presence and refocus on your breathing.

2. Walking Meditation: Find a quiet place where you can walk with no distractions or interruptions. It could be a short distance or one that is longer with turns and obstructions. Start walking slowly and focus on every movement your body makes, be it standing, balancing, stepping, or changing direction. Mentally zero-in on the muscles it takes to make these movements. If your thoughts wander, acknowledge them and refocus on the movements related to walking.

3. Body Scan Meditation: Lie on your back with your legs extended and arms to your side, palms up. Focus your attention on each part of your body one at a time– head to toes, or toes to head. As you go from part to part, flex those muscles and hold for a few seconds Then completely relax the muscles. Acknowledge any thoughts, emotions, or feelings that arise at each point and refocus. When finished, totally relax the body and breathe.

4. Recipe Meditation: Decide what recipe to prepare and obtain a printed copy. Gather all the necessary ingredients. As you mix them, focus on each ingredient and attempt to experience it with as many

senses as you can: touch, taste, smell, sight, feel, and sound. When completely finished with the preparation, attempt to experience each ingredient again individually while eating the finished meal.

5. Tai Chi and Yoga: Research and find a Tai Chi or yoga class taught by a seasoned professional. Sign up and attend at least six sessions (one per week). Practice what you learned each day for a minimum of 10 to 15 minutes.

6. Mindful Gazing: Sit comfortably and take a few deep breaths. Now visually focus (don't stare) on an object that stays somewhat consistent. Blank out everything else. If your mind wanders, bring it back to the object at hand and breathe slowly and consistently. It is good to start by doing this for 5 to 10 minutes.

(Author's note: My favorite focus point is a flame from a candle or fire pit.)

In Conclusion:

Mindfulness is about generating a heightened sense of awareness of our surroundings. There are so many opportunities to be mindful, but we must be open to them, aware of them, and perceive how they affect us and those around us. If we can focus on the present moment, being fully aware of everything we do, we can let go of any concerns of the future or anxieties over the past. This can produce more fulfilling relationships and interactions, as well as increase productivity.

If you ever find yourself trying to remember if you paid a bill, or you sometimes forget why you walked into a certain room, you may be showing signs that you have a lot going on in your mind. It could be an indication that you need to slow down, relax, and refocus your life.

Just like anything else worth pursuing, mindfulness takes effort and practice. It takes time to develop. Few are effective at it at first. Your mind will probably wander to persistent thoughts of what you need to do, should do in the future, or should've done in the past. But be patient. With repetition, you'll get better at adhering to the now and will soon realize you are living a more peaceful life with less stress. You will also notice improved relationships, better mental health, and greater overall happiness. It's worth it!

"If you are depressed, you are living in the past. If you are anxious, you are living in the future. If you are at peace, you are living in the present."

–Lao Tzu
Ancient Chinese Philosopher

Part Three

Ease into Aging

BRINGING IT ALL HOME:
THE BALL IS IN YOUR COURT

"If you could kick the person in the pants responsible for most of your troubles, you wouldn't sit for a month."

–Theodore Roosevelt
Statesman, Conservationist, Writer,
and the 26th U.S. President

L ife has a way of throwing us curveballs. It can get very complicated if we aren't prepared. Obviously, we cannot be ready for everything, but we can take action and make adjustments that will lessen the impact, particularly of those things that can be predicted as likely.

Over the years we receive many signals and signs of things to come. We get them from our genetic makeup and from our family tendencies, but most occurrences are the result of our own decisions.

The key is to be open and aware of what life is telling us early enough to give us the opportunity to make adjustments or corrections. Many of the challenges we have later in life can be avoided, or at least minimized, if we take the necessary steps to deal with them.

Life expectancy has increased. This means we should have more years to enjoy the fruits of our labor and live more fulfilling lives. But we need to make sure we take care of ourselves. No one wants to live a long life only to spend a good portion of it unable to enjoy the time.

Many of the problems that can haunt us in our mature years have much earlier roots, so it's imperative we recognize them and work at reducing their effects while there is still an opportunity to do so (i.e., before the worst is inevitable). It is obviously much better to deal with the issues before they become a factor…or even sooner, preventatively. We all age differently, and at different times. On top of that, we all have different needs and desires for ourselves and those around us. It is always good to confer with others, especially those who have gone through challenges and could provide insight. That being said, we know and understand ourselves better than anyone else does. We know what motivates us. We know what makes us tick. We know our strengths and weaknesses, as well as our goals and dreams. It is important to pocket and use the knowledge and the inspiration received from others, but also to rely on our own instincts.

How do you know what adjustments to make when the need to make changes isn't totally evident? You play the odds. That's right. But this isn't a real gamble, as by being proactive, you may be able to control the odds! There is so much information available today to help individuals understand the aging process, allowing people to address the effects and even conquer many of them. At the touch of a keyboard, you can research a multitude of material and use it to better yourself. But you have to know what to look for and where to start. You have to make a plan in each area of your life and stick to it. That's the whole purpose of *Ease into Aging: The Guide.*

It's your life. Take charge!

266

*

*A portion of proceeds from the sale of this book
will be used to benefit the kids at*
ST JUDE'S CHILDREN'S RESEARCH HOSPITAL.

****

If you love **Ease into Aging: The Guide,**
please go to www.Amazon.com,
enter **Ease into Aging: The Guide** *or*
scan with camera, the code below, and
write a review.

Forever Grateful!
– Dick

Appendix

Included in the Appendix are four assessments, mentioned in Chapter One and Chapter Two, that help the reader in the decision-making and planning process for the upcoming years. These can assist with goal setting and considering which areas to direct efforts first. Fill these items out as completely and accurately as possible. You may need assistance, so take time to discuss the results with those who have "skin in the game," such as immediate family members or a spouse. You may also solicit opinions from many of your trusted advisors.

***Ease Into Aging*: Where I Am Now Assessment**

Answer these questions as accurately as possible in order to have a picture of your life today. The responses are for your eyes only.

Age:________ Weight:________ Height: _________

BMI: ________*

Resting Heart Rate: ________** Marital Status: ________

Number of Parents Alive: ________ Deceased: ________

Children Alive: ________ Children Deceased: ________

Dependent(s): _________

Siblings Alive: ________ Siblings Deceased: ________

Cause(s) of death or debilitation for the above individuals:

____

____

____

Family Income _____________ Occupation: _______________

Spouse's Occupation: _____________

Education Level _________ Housing Costs Per Year: _________

Rent/Own:_________

Current Debt (e.g., credit card, loan, mortgage, car): _________

Savings: _________

Net Worth: ___________***

Have a 4-6 Month Emergency Fund? Y N

Retirement provisions made and assets:

____

____

____

Hobbies? Y N They are:

____

____

____

Time spent doing hobbies (on average) per week over a
month: _____________

Health problems (list):

____

____

____

Alcohol Servings: ______per week   ______per day

How Much TV Per Day? ____________

Approx. Date of Last Full Physical Exam: _________

Dental Check Up: _________

Church Member? Y N   Social Organizations? Y N

Life Insurance? Y N   How much? ___________

Health Insurance? Y N

Strenuous Exercise Per Week (hours): Cardio: _________

Resistance: _________

Truly Close Friends: Y N   How Many? ________

On Average, the Number of Times Per Day You Can Truly Relax________

Last Time Travelled for Pleasure and Relaxation: ________
Number of Days: ________

Location Visited: ____________________

Activities: ____

Percent That My Time is Under My Control ________%

***Find by calculating: (Weight in pounds/Height in inches-squared) x 703**
****Find pulse for 15 seconds and multiply by four.**
*****Total assets minus total debt.**

Ease into Aging: Definitions for Life Assessment

Find a quiet, comfortable place to relax and define what the following terms really mean to you. Don't worry about specifics and use as few words as possible while completing this exercise. Use your own thoughts.

1. Success:

____

____

____

____

2. Financial Freedom:

____

____

____

____

3. Good Health:

____

____

____

____

4. Social Acceptance:

____

____

____

____

5. Mental Health:

____

____

____

____

6. Happiness:

____

____

____

____

7. Spirituality:

____

____

<hr>

<hr>

274

8. Intelligence:

<hr>

<hr>

<hr>

<hr>

Ease Into Aging: **Strengths And Weaknesses Survey**

The following are personality qualities that could be of benefit as you progress through life. Rate yourself from one to five on each trait (i.e., five being the highest). Don't overanalyze, but be honest, and ask others who are close to you to assist. This exercise will help you to understand yourself better and have a more accurate picture of how others perceive you. Plus, it will be fun!

1. Persistent	1	2	3	4	5
2. Adaptable	1	2	3	4	5
3. Task-Oriented	1	2	3	4	5
4. Insightful	1	2	3	4	5
5. Organized	1	2	3	4	5
6. Appearance-Driven	1	2	3	4	5
7. Perseverant	1	2	3	4	5
8. Future-Driven	1	2	3	4	5
9. Peaceful or Content	1	2	3	4	5
10. Compassionate	1	2	3	4	5
11. Empathetic	1	2	3	4	5
12. Sympathetic	1	2	3	4	5
13. Goal-Oriented	1	2	3	4	5
14. Enthusiastic	1	2	3	4	5
15. Persuasive	1	2	3	4	5
16. Happy	1	2	3	4	5
17. Research-Oriented	1	2	3	4	5
18. Technology-Fluent	1	2	3	4	5

19. Ability to Relax	1	2	3	4	5
20. Health Conscious	1	2	3	4	5
21. Spiritual	1	2	3	4	5
22. Family-Oriented	1	2	3	4	5
23. Flexible	1	2	3	4	5
24. Decision-Oriented	1	2	3	4	5
25. Accepting	1	2	3	4	5
26. Humorous	1	2	3	4	5
27. Curious	1	2	3	4	5
28. Humble	1	2	3	4	5
29. Positive-Thinking	1	2	3	4	5
30. Grateful	1	2	3	4	5
31. Confident	1	2	3	4	5
32. Honest	1	2	3	4	5
33. Loyal	1	2	3	4	5
34. Detail-Oriented	1	2	3	4	5
35. Driven	1	2	3	4	5

Total ___________

Add up your ratings and apply your total score to the following:

165-175	You probably overestimated your qualities!
145-165	You are probably living a very fulfilling life!
100-145	Put your strengths to work for a better future.
35-100	Focus on your weaknesses and make meaningful changes.

Ease into Aging: Goal-Setting Checklist

A goal is only a wish unless you write it down and intentionally pursue it. Use this checklist to state your goals in the following aspects of life. Then calculate a timeframe and formulate four strategies to achieve each goal. It is a good idea to keep this list handy so that you remain focused on your plan and the desired outcomes. Once you achieve one goal, create a new one so that you can build on your success and keep growing!

<u>Financial</u>

Goal:

____

____

____

____

Time frame: 1 year   5 years   10 years

Other: ___________

Strategies:

1. ______________________________________

2. ______________________________________

3. ______________________________________

4. ____

<u>Health and Fitness</u>

Goal:

____

____

____

____

Time frame: 1 year   5 years   10 years

Other: _________

Strategies:

1. ____

2. ____

3. ____

4. ____

<u>Interpersonal Relationships</u>

Goal:

____

____

____

____

Time frame: 1 year   5 years   10 years

Other: __________

Strategies:

1. ____

2. ____

3. ____

4. ____

<u>Occupation or Retirement</u>

Goal:

____

____

____

____

Time frame: 1 year   5 years   10 years

Other: _____________

Strategies:

1. ____

2. ____

3. ____

4. ____

<u>Personal Growth</u> (whatever this means to you)

Goal:

____

____

____

____

Time frame: 1 year   5 years   10 years

Other: _____________

Strategies:

1. ____

2. ____

3. ____

4. ____

Books

The following is a list of books I read and studied while growing up, as an adult, and in trying to be a more functional part of society. This list is ever changing and continues to grow…as do I! For a more up-to-date list, feel free to contact me at: www.DickHartman.com or dickhartman2020@gmail.com.

Chicken Soup for The Soul, by Jack Canfield, et al.

This is a series of books with short selections and stories meant to uplift, inspire, and encourage reflection. Each book contains writings about life that will make you think, laugh, and cry. The items are easy and quick to read, and they can be enjoyed by reading straight through or by skipping around. These books are also a great read-aloud option for families.

Communication: The Missing Piece of the Marriage Puzzle, by Steve and Debbie Wilson

This is one of my favorite books for couples. It explains the role that communication plays in people's lives and helps spouses communicate more effectively.

Don't Sweat the Small Stuff, by Richard Carlson

This book reminds individuals how not to get bogged down with the minutiae of life for a more content and peaceful approach.

Everyday Millionaires, by Chris Hogan

This must-read book, from a Dave Ramsey disciple, dispels myths about millionaires and explains how the reader can become wealthy…and stay that way.

Facing Your Giants, by Max Lucado

This awe-inspiring guide uses the story of David and Goliath to help readers find strategies to overcome adversity.

How to Win Friends and Influence People, by Dale Carnegie

This is my second all-time favorite book. It didn't teach anything I didn't already know about dealing with people, but it drove home the importance of approaching people and topics the right way.

Life Strategies: Doing What Works, Doing What Matters, by Phillip McGraw, Ph.D. (Dr. Phil)

This book provides a straightforward approach to living life to its fullest and not being trapped in our own misgivings.

Motivating the Unmotivated, by Dick Hartman

Yep, that's me! This was my first book, written early during my career in education. It's designed to help parents and educators teach teenagers to be all-around better people and attain more from life.

Sacred Hoops, by Phil Jackson

This venerable and well-respected professional basketball coach shares his unusual but highly effective approach to life and how it meshed with his career and role in motivating others.

The 5 Love Languages, *by* Gary Chapman

This is a great primer for all couples, whether newlywed or celebrating many years together. It teaches how and why spouses communicate the way they do with each other.

Top Screwups Doctors Make and How to Avoid Them, by Joe and Teresa Graedon

These best-selling health authors and teachers explain how to take charge of your health and not fall prey to the mistakes others make.

The Art of War, by Sun Tzu

This all-time classic was written over 2500 years ago and draws interesting parallels between engaging in war and living a peaceful life.

The Purpose Driven Life, by Rick Warren

These prophetic words, from a pastor's perspective, explain why we are here and how to make the best of our time on earth.

The Inner Game of Tennis, by Tim Gallwey

The author compares the game of tennis to life with some very interesting insights about behaviors and their outcomes.

The Way of The Wizard, by Deepak Chopra

In this book, an ancient wizard (Merlin) guides readers on a successful path for the present day. While the premise may seem a little cheesy, the words are still very meaningful.

Think and Grow Rich, by Napoleon Hill

This is a timeless classic that explains how each person has the power to grow and control his or her own measure of wealth.

Undeniable Secrets of Marriage, by Allen Hunt, Ph.D.

This is a must-read guide about how to take your relationship to a new level.

The 7 ***Habits of Highly Effective People,*** by Stephen Covey

From one of the most respected authors in the world, this book helps individuals step up to the next level, *whatever that means personally.*

The New Toughness Training for Sports, by James E. Loehr, Ed.D.

As one the world's premier sports psychologists, the author presents, explains, and develops mental, emotional, and physical conditioning techniques that have helped many athletes reach greater heights in their chosen areas.

The Bible

Regardless of your religious or spiritual orientation, *The Bible* is a great manual for living life and keeping your eyes on the ultimate prize–whatever that means to you. It remains a great source of guidance and inspiration for people across the world.

You, Staying Young, by Mehmet Oz, M.D. and Michael Roizen, M.D.

This is a great read that describes in simple language how our bodies work and how to minimize problems that can arise over the years.

You, The Owner's Manual, by Mehmet Oz, M.D. and Michael Roizen, M.D.

This all-encompassing manual is meant to help readers become and remain healthier and more functional throughout life.

Zig Ziglar, Dave Ramsey, Denis Waitley, Steve and Debbie Wilson, Scot Hahn, Max Lucado, Suze Orman, Jordan Peterson, Kurt Warner, Les Brown, and Greg and Erin Smalley.

Quotations

Any quotations used in this book were obtained through Brainyquotes.com unless otherwise noted.

Introductory quotation:

Lucado, M. (1996) *God's Little Inspirational Book.* Dallas: Word Publishing, Inc., p 153

REFERENCES

Administration on Aging. (2020, October 15). *How Much Care Will You Need?* U.S. Department of Health and Human Services. https://longtermcare.acl.gov/the-basics/how-much-care-will-you-need.html

Anger Management: Your Questions Answered. (2020, March 5). Healthy Lifestyle: Adult Health. Mayo Clinic. Retrieved November 2020 from: https://www.mayoclinic.org/healthy-lifestyle/adult-health/in-depth/anger-management/art-20048149

Bay Pines Veterans Hospital Staff Representative (Personal Communication, January 2020). Effects of alcoholism.

Caffeine: How Much is Too Much? (2020 March 26). Healthy Lifestyle: Nutrition and Healthy Eating. Mayo Clinic. Retrieved October 2020 from: https://www.mayoclinic.org/healthy-lifestyle/nutrition-and-healthy-eating/in-depth/caffeine/art-20045678

Davison, K. W. and Mostofsky, E. (2010). Anger Expression and Risk of Coronary Heart Disease: Evidence from the Nova Scotia Heath Survey. *American Heart Journal,* 159(2), 199-206. https://doi.org/10.1016/j.ahj.2009.11.007

Dixit, J. (2008, November 1). The Art of Now: Six Steps to Living in the Moment Today. *Psychology Today.* https://www.psychologytoday.com/us/articles/200811/the-art-now-six-steps-living-in-the-moment

Enright, Robert. (2017, September 18). Anger and Cancer: Is There a Relationship? *Psychology Today.* https://www.psychologytoday.com/us/blog/the-forgiving-life/201709/anger-and-cancer-is-there-relationship

Exercise and Stress: Get Moving to Manage Stress. (2020, August 18). Healthy Lifestyle: Stress Management. The Mayo Clinic. Retrieved November 2020 from: https://www.mayoclinic.org/healthy-lifestyle/stress-management/in-depth/exercise-and-stress/art-20044469

Ferguson, Sian. (2019 Oct. 28). *Is Sex Important in a Relationship? 12 Things to Consider.* Healthline Media. https://www.healthline.com/health/healthy-sex/is-sex-important-in-a-relationship

Fung, J. M.D. (2016). *The Obesity Code: Unlocking the Secrets of Weight Loss.* Vancouver: Greystone Books.

Fung, J. M.D. and Moore, J. (2016) *The Complete Guide to Fasting: Heal Your Body Through Intermittent, Alternate-Day, and Extended Fasting. L*as Vegas: Victory Belt.

How Likely are You to Need Long-Term Care? (2016, February 24). ElderLawAnswers.Com. Retrieved August 2020 from: https://www.elderlawanswers.com/how-likely-are-you-to-need-long-term-care–15501

Hui, L., Waite, L. J., & Shen, S. (2016) Is Sex Good for Your Health? A National Study on Partnered Sexuality and Cardiovascular Risk Among Older Men and Women. Journal of Health and Social Behavior, 57(3), 276-296. https://doi.org/10.1177/0022146516661597

Know Your Teeth: Improve Your Oral Health in 2011. (2011, December). The Academy of General Dentistry. Retrieved August 2020 from: http://knowyourteeth.com/print/printpreview.asp?content=article&abc=H&iid=184&aid=8674

Laino, Charlene. (2016, June 4) *Chocolate Milk Refuels Muscles After Workout.* WebMD. https://www.webmd.com/fitness-exercise/news/20100604/chocolate-milk-refuels-muscles-after-workout

Lockett, E. (2019, August 29). *Weighted Blankets: Do They Work?* Healthline Media. https://www.healthline.com/health/anxiety/do-weighted-blankets-work

Martin, E. (2019, January 9). *The Government Shutdown Spotlights a Bigger Issue: Nearly 78% of U.S. Workers Live Paycheck to Paycheck.* CNBC: Money. https://www.cnbc.com/2019/01/09/shutdown-highlights-that-4-in-5-us-workers-live-paycheck-to-paycheck.html

Milner, C. E. and Cote, K. A. (2009). Benefits of Napping in Healthy Adults: Impact of Nap Length, Time of Day, Age, and Experience with Napping. *Journal of Sleep Research*, 18(2), 272-281. https://onlinelibrary.wiley.com/doi/full/10.1111/j.1365-2869.2008.00718.x

National Academies of Sciences, Engineering, and Medicine. (2020). *Social Isolation and Loneliness in Older Adults: Opportunities for the Health Care System.* The National Academies Press. [PDF] https://doi.org/10.17226/2566

NFL Combine Trainer: 225 Bench Press for Enduring Strength. (2017, August 11). BodyBuilding.com. Retrieved October 2020 from: https://www.bodybuilding.com/fun/nfl-combine-trainer-225-bench-press.html

Picchi, A. (2020, February 12). Here's a Top Reason Americans are Carrying an Average Credit Card Balance of Over $6200. *USA Today*. https://www.usatoday.com/story/money/2020/02/12/credit-card-debt-average-balance-hits-6-200-and-limit-31-000/4722897002/

ACKNOWLEDGEMENTS

I won't bore you with a laundry list of people who contributed to the start or completion of this project, but I would like to recognize a few special individuals who helped and inspired me to write *Ease into Aging: The Guide.*

Lee Caldecutt: My editor. Besides her ability to organize, make suggestions, and correct a multitude of errors, she was able to give me more in-depth insight from other viewpoints: namely the feminine side and those of other age groups.

Eric: My son. His undying devotion and loyalty to his family has always inspired and influenced me. If you read closely, you probably noticed that he is ultimately the person who inspired me to put my knowledge and expertise out for the world to see.

Betty: My amazing wife of many years. Her loyalty and undying love constantly inspire me to be a better person. During the process of putting this book together, she kept me motivated and helped me past many obstacles, reminding me that God was in charge and in control.

Notes

Dick Hartman has worn many hats throughout his working career. As a coach, he received Coach of the Year honors fourteen times and led the top male tennis team in his county's history, while also winning twelve district championships and one state title. Additionally, he developed a successful real estate business and other entrepreneurial initiatives, implementing many of the life skills and strategies described in this book.

A community leader, mentor, author, teacher, speaker, and coach, Dick has honed many interpersonal skills and strategies to help others seek and reach their potential while getting the most out of life's experiences and opportunities. His first book, Motivating the Unmotivated, applies a practical, pragmatic, but loving approach to reaching teens, helping them achieve and take ownership of their success during those difficult years. He believes in bringing a dogged determination and commitment to the table in all pursuits, and he is a tireless advocate for continuous learning and personal growth–at any age.

Dick presently lives in Central Florida with his beautiful wife, Betty, who has put up with him for a very long time. He has one adult son and three grandchildren. A self-described "rabid sports fan," he also enjoys fitness training, biking, kayaking and international travel.

When he is not writing, Dick can be found immersed in his community and enjoying time with his family. He serves as a lector and leader at his church and has been an active member on a number of advisory boards throughout the years.

Made in the USA
Columbia, SC
10 February 2021